Essential
New Zealand

AAA Publishing 1000 AAA Drive, Heathrow, Florida 32746

New Zealand: Regions and Best places to see

 Best places to see 34–55

 Featured sight

Original text by Allan Edie
Updated by Susi Bailey

Edited, designed and produced by AA Publishing
© AA Media Limited 2010
Maps © AA Media Limited 2010

ISBN: 978-1-59508-374-6

Published in the United States by AAA Publishing,
1000 AAA Drive, Heathrow, Florida 32746
Published in the United Kingdom by AA Publishing

Color separation: MRM Graphics Ltd
Printed and bound in Italy by Printer Trento S.r.l.

A04015
Maps in this title produced from map data © New Holland Publishing (South Africa) (PTY) Limited 2009

About this book

Symbols are used to denote the following categories:

✚ map reference to maps on cover

✉ address or location

☎ telephone number

🕐 opening times

✋ admission charge

🍴 restaurant or café on premises or nearby

Ⓜ nearest underground train station

🚌 nearest bus/tram route

🚉 nearest overground train station

⛴ nearest ferry stop

✈ nearest airport

❓ other practical information

ℹ tourist information office

► indicates the page where you will find a fuller description

This book is divided into five sections:

The essence of New Zealand
pages 6–19
Introduction; Features; Food and drink; Short break

Planning pages 20–33
Before you go; Getting there; Getting around; Being there

Best places to see pages 34–55
The unmissable highlights of any visit to New Zealand

Best things to do pages 56–69
Great places to have lunch; Adventure activities; Stunning views; Places to take the children and more

Exploring pages 70–185
The best places to visit in New Zealand, organized by area

Maps

All map references are to the maps on the covers. For example, Christchurch has the reference ✚ 5S – indicating the grid square in which it is to be found

Admission prices

Inexpensive (under NZ$10)
Moderate (NZ$10–$30)
Expensive (over NZ$30)

Hotel prices

Prices are per room per night:
$ inexpensive (NZ$100)
$$ moderate (NZ$100–$200)
$$$ expensive to luxury (over NZ$200)

Restaurant prices

Price for a three-course meal per person without drinks or service:
$ inexpensive (under NZ$40)
$$ moderate (NZ$40–$60)
$$$ expensive (over NZ$60)

Contents

The essence of...

The scenic beauty of New Zealand is well known. In many places the landscape is a dramatic mixture of mountains, glaciers, fjords and turbulent rivers, yet there are also gentle fields of grass, evergreen forests and quiet lakes. For many visitors, touring the countryside in a car or long-distance bus, or admiring the views through a window, glass in hand, is pleasure enough. However, over the last 20 years or so New Zealand has also become established as a destination for action, renowned for 'soft' adventure and for more spectacular thrill experiences. Concern for the environment and a yearning for healthy pursuits have increased worldwide, making New Zealand a popular destination for enjoying a host of outdoor activities.

features

According to tradition, the early Polynesian Maori peoples were the first human beings to inhabit New Zealand, arriving at the islands in fleets of canoes during the 10th to 14th centuries. They were followed by European explorers, whalers and sealers, and in the 19th century settlers and soldiers, gold-miners and opportunists arrived. Today, tourists come from all over the world.

Tourism New Zealand promotes the country as '100% Pure New Zealand', at 'the most beautiful end of the Earth'. The organization's objective of attracting potential visitors is made easier by the simple fact that this is a country of stunning landscapes, friendly people and fascinating culture. Its job of advertising the country to an international audience has been further helped by the release of such films as the *Lord of the Rings* trilogy, *River Queen* and *Narnia*, all of which show off New Zealand's natural beauty in a way that has captured imaginations worldwide. This is one of the world's most desirable travel destinations. With its easy-going lifestyle, clean, uncrowded environment, and spectacular landscapes ranging from volcanoes to glaciers, New Zealand surely is a blessed country.

GEOGRAPHY
The total area of New Zealand is 270,500sq km (105,500sq miles), of which two islands, the North and South, comprise 98 per cent. The South Island is a third larger than the North, but the North claims three-quarters of the population – including the largest city, Auckland, and the capital of Wellington. Stewart Island, 30km (20 miles) south of the South Island, is the third-largest land mass at about 1,700sq km (650sq miles). No part of New Zealand is farther than 130km (80 miles) from the sea. The coastline, 15,000km (9,300 miles) long, includes islands, harbours and estuaries.

THE CLIMATE
Summer lasts from December to February and fine autumn weather usually lasts through to May. During the winter months (June to August) there is more rain, and snow falls in the high country of the North and South islands.

THE PEOPLE
Total population is 4.3 million, around 70 per cent of which is of European descent – mainly from Britain. The indigenous Polynesian people, called Maori, make up 15 per cent. Other South Pacific peoples and Asians make up most of the rest. Some 85 per cent of the population are urban dwellers.

TIME AND PLACE
New Zealand lies in the temperate belt of the South Pacific Ocean; the 45th parallel (halfway between the Equator and the South Pole) passes through the South Island. In longitude it's almost exactly opposite the UK.

Standard time is 12 hours ahead of GMT; from early October until late March daylight-saving advances the time by one hour.

food & drink

New Zealand has cast off its image as a country of meat pies and lamb roasts, and offers a huge range of dining options, from top restaurants to Maori *hangi* (► 33), international eateries and small cafés serving freshly prepared innovative dishes using local produce. To drink, there are, of course, plenty of award-winning wines to choose from.

The international fast-food chains are well represented and takeaway (food-to-go) places are common. Many shopping malls also have a food court offering a selection of cheap light meals.

MEAT

Lamb is the traditional meat of New Zealand, usually served roasted with mint sauce or jelly, but beef, pork and chicken are all popular. Canterbury lamb is esteemed. Hogget is one-year-old (the tenderest) lamb.

Barbecues are something of a Kiwi institution, and many parks and beach reserves have public barbecue facilities where you can cook up a steak.

SEAFOOD

Seafood delicacies are widely available. These include Nelson scallops, Marlborough and Coromandel mussels, Bluff (deep-sea) oysters from the far south of the South Island and West Coast whitebait.

Fish dishes make use of snapper, orange roughy, hapuka (grouper), flounder, blue cod and John Dory. Salmon are reared in the south but trout, although a popular game-fish, is not caught commercially, nor offered in restaurants.

FRUIT AND VEGETABLES

A wide variety of locally grown vegetables is available, from supermarkets or direct from the growers, where prices are generally lower and the produce fresher. Kumara is a native

sweet potato. Seasonal, local fresh fruit includes apples, peaches, pears, plums, apricots and berries.

The prickly skinned kiwi fruit was known as Chinese gooseberry until the Kiwis decided to market it as their own. The gold-fleshed variety is produced exclusively by Zespri.

DESSERTS

Fresh strawberries, raspberries and boysenberries are summer favourites, served with creamy New Zealand ice cream, and in places you can 'pick your own' fruit straight from the vine. The dessert New Zealanders claim as their own (although Australians disagree with this) is pavlova, a meringue base covered with a layer of whipped cream and topped with fresh fruit.

DRINK

New Zealand's tap water is perfectly safe to drink, although bottled water is popular. Water from streams and lakes should be purified before drinking. Tea is an essential part of Kiwi hospitality, while good coffee is available in cafés. Fresh milk and fruit juice are inexpensive.

Traditionally, New Zealanders are a nation of beer drinkers and, while brands like DB, Lion and Steinlager dominate, many local boutique-brewery labels have added interest to the market.

New Zealand wines are now well established internationally, with Marlborough Sauvignon Blancs and Otago Pinot Noirs acclaimed in particular. Leading labels include Cloudy Bay and Montana.

MEAL TIMES

Kiwis usually have a light breakfast and lunch, and a substantial evening meal ('dinner' or 'tea'), eaten between 6pm and 8pm. Most motel rooms have cooking facilities, but a continental breakfast can be provided on request.

short break

If you have only a short time to visit New Zealand and would like to take home some unforgettable memories, you can do something local and capture the real flavour of the islands. The following suggestions will give you a wide range of sights and experiences that won't take very long, won't cost you very much and will make your visit very special.

● **Take a hike:** follow a city walk, hike through native bush, or trek for a week among stunning scenery.

● **Go horse trekking:** explore the high country on horseback, or gallop along a beach.

- **Visit a museum:** notable museums can be found in Auckland, Wellington, Christchurch and Dunedin.

- **Inspect a thermal area:** see bubbling mud and spouting geysers, or soak in hot-water pools. There are many thermal spas in the North Island and two main resorts in the South Island.

- **Eat a New Zealand delicacy:** special dishes include Bluff oysters, Nelson scallops, West Coast whitebait, Canterbury lamb and pavlova dessert.

- **Watch a Maori concert:** learn more about Maori culture by going to a *kapa haka* (dance and music) show, and then follow it with a traditional *hangi* meal (▶ 33).

● **Ride a jet-boat:** fast rides on rivers and lakes are one of the country's many thrilling adventures.

● **Stroll along a beach:** west coast beaches can be wild at any season; safe swimming beaches abound in the rest of the country.

● **Watch a rugby match or go horse racing:** both exemplify the sporting passion of Kiwis.

● **Drink the local wine or beer:** try a chilled Sauvignon Blanc, or an ice-cold beer: there are many award-winning labels to choose from and places to try them.

● **Weekend markets:** most cities have a Saturday or Sunday market selling fresh fruit, crafts and sundries. These are great places to meet New Zealanders at their most relaxed.

Planning

Before you go

WHEN TO GO

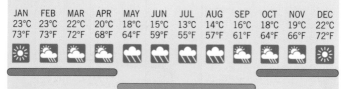

JAN	FEB	MAR	APR	MAY	JUN	JUL	AUG	SEP	OCT	NOV	DEC
23°C	23°C	22°C	20°C	18°C	15°C	13°C	14°C	16°C	18°C	19°C	22°C
73°F	73°F	72°F	68°F	64°F	59°F	55°F	57°F	61°F	64°F	66°F	72°F

🔵 High season 🔵 Low season

New Zealand's summer lasts from December through February, although November and March can also be hot. The peak period for visitors is summer, which is when many festivals are held and most Kiwis also take their annual holiday. As a result, accommodation and sights tend to be busy. The winter ski season (Jun–Sep) attracts visitors to resorts on Mount Ruapehu and in the Southern Alps.

WHAT YOU NEED

		UK	Germany	USA	Canada	Australia	Ireland	Netherlands	Spain
● Required	Some countries require a passport to remain valid for a minimum period (usually at least six months) beyond the date of entry – check before you travel.								
○ Suggested									
▲ Not required									
Passport (or National Identity Card where applicable)		●	●	●	●	●	●	●	●
Visa (regulations can change – check before you travel)		▲	▲	▲	▲	▲	▲	▲	▲
Onward or Return Ticket		●	●	●	●	●	●	●	●
Health Inoculations		▲	▲	▲	▲	▲	▲	▲	▲
Health Documentation (▶ 23, Health Insurance)		○	○	○	○	○	○	○	○
Travel Insurance		○	○	○	○	○	○	○	○
Driving Licence (national)		●	●	●	●	●	●	●	●
Car Insurance Certificate		▲	▲	▲	▲	▲	▲	▲	▲
Car Registration Document		▲	▲	▲	▲	▲	▲	▲	▲

WEBSITES

● www.aatravel.co.nz
Visitor information site of New Zealand Automobile Association.

● www.destination-nz.com
Online travel guide, with accommodation and sights.

● www.doc.govt.nz
Department of Conservation
website, with information on
national and other parks.

● www.newzealand.com
Official website of Tourism
New Zealand.

● www.i-site.org
Lists Tourism New Zealand's
visitor centres around the
country.

● www.tourism.net.nz
Lists over 12,000 New Zealand
tourism and travel sites.

TOURIST OFFICES AT HOME
In the UK
Tourism New Zealand
New Zealand House
80 Haymarket
London
SW1Y 4QT
☎ 020 7930 1662;
www.newzealand.com

In the USA
Tourism New Zealand
Suite 2510
222 East 41st Street
New York
NY10017
☎ 212/661-7088;
www.newzealand.com

HEALTH INSURANCE
Some emergency medical services are subsidized for visitors from
Australia and the UK, but all visitors are strongly recommended to arrange
medical insurance coverage before their trip.

TIME DIFFERENCES

GMT	New Zealand	Germany	USA (NY)	Netherlands	Spain
12 noon	12 midnight	1PM	7AM	1PM	1PM

New Zealand standard time is 12 hours ahead of Greenwich Mean Time
(GMT+12). New Zealand's proximity to the International Date Line makes
it one of the first countries to see each new day.

NATIONAL HOLIDAYS

1–2 Jan *New Year*
6 Feb *Waitangi Day*
Mar/Apr *Good Friday*
Mar/Apr *Easter Monday*
25 Apr *ANZAC Day*
Jun (first Mon) *Queen's Birthday*
Oct (fourth Mon) *Labour Day*
25 Dec *Christmas Day*
26 Dec *Boxing Day*

Most stores and attractions are closed on Christmas Day, Good Friday and the morning of ANZAC Day. Tourist amenities are usually open on the other public holidays.

You will also find that there are regional holidays during the year, corresponding to the founding days of each of the country's 13 provinces. The main ones are:
Wellington region: third Monday in January.
Auckland, Bay of Islands, Rotorua and Taupo: last Monday in January.
Christchurch: during Cup and Show Week in November.
Queenstown and Dunedin: last Monday in March.

WHAT'S ON WHEN

January *Auckland Anniversary Regatta,* Auckland: the world's largest one-day sailing regatta is held on Waitemata Harbour (last Monday in January). *World Buskers Festival,* Christchurch: features international acts.

February *Wine Marlborough Festival,* Blenheim, Marlborough (second or third weekend of February).

February/March *International Arts Festival,* Wellington (biennial, in even years).

March *Golden Shears sheep-shearing competition,* Masterton. *Ellerslie International Flower Show,* Christchurch: held over five days (second week).
Wild Foods Festival, Hokitika.

Easter *Royal Easter Show,* Auckland.

April *Warbirds over Wanaka,* Wanaka: the largest aviation show in the southern hemisphere (biennial, in even years).

June *National Agricultural Fieldays,* Hamilton: one of the world's largest agricultural shows, held over four days at Mystery Creek (second week of the month).

June/July *Winter Festival,* Queenstown: a ten-day festival marking the start of the ski season.

September *Blossom Festival,* Alexandra. *World of Wearable Art Festival,* Wellington.

October *Taranaki Rhododendron and Garden Festival,* New Plymouth: takes place over a week.

November *Cup and Show Week,* Christchurch (mid-November). *Guy Fawkes evening,* countrywide: fireworks on 5 November.

Getting there

BY AIR

Auckland, North Island

21km (13 miles) to city centre

N/A
50 minutes
40 minutes

Christchurch, South Island

12km (7 miles) to city centre

N/A
30 minutes
20 minutes

Most visitors arrive by air, through the three main international airports of Auckland, Wellington and Christchurch. Auckland Airport (☎ 09 275 0789; www.auckland-airport.co.nz) is the country's largest gateway. Airbus Express operates from the international terminal every 15 or 20 minutes during the day and half-hourly from 7:45pm, daily 5:20am–10:15pm. The domestic terminal (follow the blue line on the pavement), serving Air New Zealand and Qantas, is a 10-minute walk from the international terminal; a free shuttle bus connects them, running every 20 minutes daily 6am–10:30pm.

Wellington Airport (☎ 04 385 5100; www.wlg-airport.co.nz) mainly handles flights from New Zealand and Australian destinations and is 8km (5 miles) from the city. Airport Flyer buses connect the terminal with downtown stops every 20 or 30 minutes Mon–Fri 6:20am–8:30pm, and half-hourly or hourly Sat–Sun 6:50am–8:50pm.

Christchurch Airport (☎ 03 358 5029; www.christchurchairport.co.nz) is 12km (7 miles) from the city. The Red Bus City Flyer operates between the terminal and the city half-hourly or hourly Mon–Fri 5:52am–1am, Sat 7:04am–12:55am, Sun 8:05am–12:55am.

The national airline is Air New Zealand (☎ 09 357 3000; www.airnewzealand.co.nz). It flies between New Zealand and the UK, Australia, USA and various other destinations, and in addition connects all major centres within the country via a domestic network. There are also some smaller air services operating short hops and scenic flights.

Getting around

PUBLIC TRANSPORT

Regional flights Air New Zealand flies the principal routes in the country and links about 30 domestic destinations. The Star Alliance South Pacific Airpass offers flexibility on domestic flights, as well as links to Australia and Pacific Islands.

Trains TranzScenic (☎ 04 495 0775; www.tranzscenic.co.nz) operates three main rail routes: the Overlander from Auckland to Wellington; the TranzCoastal from Picton to Christchurch; and the TranzAlpine from Christchurch to Greymouth (➤ 50). Through fares are available, combining travel on rail routes and the Interislander ferry.

Coaches and buses The InterCity long-distance bus network (www.intercity.co.nz) covers much of the country; its Travelpasses are available for 1–14 days. Newmans (www.newmanscoach.co.nz) operates all major routes, and like some other companies also offers tours by long-distance bus.

Ferries The main inter-island ferry service is operated by Interislander (☎ 04 498 3302; www.interislander.co.nz). It is a roll-on roll-off service carrying passengers, motor vehicles and railroad wagons. There are several round-trip sailings from Wellington to Picton each day, taking 3 hours each way.

Urban transport Christchurch has an upgraded heritage tram system, and both it and Auckland have a good bus network. Wellington is a major transport centre and ferry terminal, with city buses as well as a cable car from downtown to the upper slopes of the Kelburn area.

FARES AND TICKETS

TranzScenic, InterCity and Interislander all have travel passes that allow you to save a lot of money. Senior citizens, young people and students are eligible for discounts with these companies.

TAXIS

Taxis can be rented from stands; they can also be flagged down. Shuttles are often better value than regular taxis for large groups. For long-distance journeys negotiate the fare in advance. You are not expected to tip taxi drivers.

DRIVING

- Speed limits on motorways: 100kph (62mph)
  Speed limits on main roads: 100kph (62mph)
  Speed limits on urban roads: 50kph (31mph)
- Vehicles drive on the left, and seatbelts must be worn in all seats where fitted at all times.
- Random breath and blood testing. Limit: 80mg (0.08g of alcohol in 100ml of blood). For drivers under 20 the limit is 30mg (0.03g) in 100ml.

- Petrol (fuel) comes in two grades: unleaded 95 octane and unleaded 91 octane. Diesel and LPG (liquefied petroleum gas) are also available. In rural areas service stations may be scarce and may be closed on weekends or outside normal hours. Major towns and cities have 24-hour stations.
- There are plenty of garages and service stations throughout the country, and most rental companies include free roadside assistance as part of the rental package. The Automobile Association in New Zealand also offers roadside assistance, plus free maps and guides (☎ 0800 500 444; www.aa.co.nz).

CAR RENTAL

All the major rental firms are represented in New Zealand. You must be at least 21 to rent a car or motor home. For inter-island travel, many companies require you to leave the vehicle on one island and pick up another after leaving the ferry. One-way rentals can also be arranged.

Being there

TOURIST OFFICES

Auckland
SkyCity, corner of Victoria
and Federal streets
☎ 09 367 6009;
www.aucklandnz.com

Wellington
Civic Square, corner of Victoria and
Wakefield streets
☎ 04 802 4860;
www.wellingtonnz.com

Christchurch
Old Chief Post Office
Cathedral Square
☎ 03 379 9629;
www.christchurchinformation.co.nz

Queenstown
Clocktower Building, corner of
Shotover and Camp streets
☎ 03 442 4100;
www.queenstown-vacation.com

Around 80 regional and local tourist
offices throughout the country form
the Visitor Information Network, co-
ordinated by Tourism New Zealand.
Because they are linked in one
network, Visitor Information
Centres, known as i-SITES, can
access information on other areas.
They provide an invaluable, up-to-
date service and should be your
first port of call.

MONEY
New Zealand currency is decimal based and
divided into dollars and cents. The New Zealand
dollar is not tied to any other currency. Coins
that are now in circulation are in denominations
of 10, 20 and 50 cents, and 1 and 2 dollars.
Notes are in denominations of 5, 10, 20, 50
and 100 dollars.

There is no limit to the amount of New
Zealand dollars that may be brought into or
taken out of the country.

Credit cards are widely accepted, including
Mastercard, Visa, American Express and Diners Club, and travellers'
cheques can be changed at banks or change bureaux in all towns.

TIPS/GRATUITIES

Tipping is not generally expected, but may be given to reward excellent service
Yes ✓   No ✕

Hotels (if service included)	✕
Restaurants (if service not included)	✕
Cafés/bars (if service not included)	✕
Taxis	✕
Tour guides	✕
Porters/ Chambermaids	✕
Toilet attendants	✕

POSTAL AND INTERNET SERVICES

The logo for NZ Post Limited is a stylized envelope. Its PostShops provide
a range of services and open Monday to Friday 9–5, with some also
opening Saturdays and Sundays.

Most hotels provide in-room Internet access. There are also
Internet cafés in most areas and public libraries with Internet.

TELEPHONES

Telecom operates the public telephone service and most call
boxes use Telecom phonecards, available from shops. For
directory enquiries dial 018, and for international directory
enquiries dial 0172. The country code for New Zealand is 64.

International dialling codes

Australia: 00 61
Germany: 00 49
Hong Kong: 00 852
Ireland: 00 353

Netherlands: 00 31
Spain: 00 34
UK: 00 44
USA and Canada: 00 1

Emergency telephone number

Police, Fire, Ambulance: 111

EMBASSIES AND CONSULATES

Australia ☎ 04 473 6411
Canada ☎ 04 473 9577
Germany ☎ 04 473 6063

Netherlands ☎ 04 471 6390
UK ☎ 04 924 2888
USA ☎ 04 462 6000

HEALTH ADVICE

The most serious potential health risk in New Zealand is from the sun. Ultra-violet radiation throughout the country is particularly high. Take adequate precautions, even on overcast days, by wearing a sun hat and using a sunscreen with a high protection factor. Always ensure that children are well protected.

Drugs Chemists (pharmacies) are usually open during normal shopping hours. If you are on unusual medication, take supplies with you as there is no guarantee that they will be available locally. Take your prescription certificate to avoid difficulties with customs.

Safe water Tap water everywhere in New Zealand is safe to drink. City water supplies are chlorinated and most are also fluoridated. If camping in remote areas, always boil water before drinking.

PERSONAL SAFETY

There is an efficient police force modelled on the British system. Police do not carry arms. While New Zealand is generally a safe society, the usual sensible precautions should be taken to ensure personal safety:

- Avoid walking alone in dark areas of towns.
- If walking in bush or mountain country, take good maps, dress sensibly, take supplies of food and drink, and tell someone what your plans are.
- Beware of pickpockets.
- Do not leave valuables in unattended cars.

ELECTRICITY

The power supply in New Zealand is 230–240 volts AC. Sockets accept two- or three-flat-pin plugs. Hotels and motels provide 110-volt/20 watt AC sockets for shavers only. An adaptor will be required for those appliances that do not operate on 230 volts.

OPENING HOURS

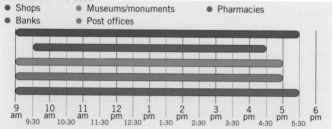

In addition to the above, pharmacies and stores are open on Saturday 9–noon or 9–4 and some shops are open on Sunday. The bigger towns usually have late-night shopping on Thursday or Friday until 8:30 or 9pm. Some smaller shops close at lunchtime on Saturdays. Local convenience stores (dairies) are usually open 7am–8pm seven days a week.

Times of museum openings vary and many are open on weekends, too – for details see individual museums listed in the Exploring section.

LANGUAGE

The common language of New Zealand is English. The written language follows British spelling convention, rather than American. There is little difference in pronunciation from one part of the country to another, except that in the south of the South Island you may detect a Scottish accent. The Maori language is undergoing a revival; you will hear it spoken on a *marae* (the area surrounding a meeting house) and on some radio stations. Visitors may also hear Maori spoken on TV and radio, used as a greeting (*kia ora*), and in place names. The language was entirely oral until early missionaries recorded it in written form. The easiest way to say Maori words is to pronounce each syllable phonetically, noting that 'wh' is pronounced 'ph'. 'Kiwi' English also tends to have its own idiosyncratic expressions or phrases.

COMMON MAORI WORDS AND PHRASES

ao cloud
Aotearoa Land of the Long White Cloud
ara path
atua god
awa river, stream
haere mai welcome
haera ra farewell
hangi a Maori feast
hau wind
Hawaiiki legendary homeland of the Maori
kia ora your good health
kumara a sweet potato
makomako bellbird
mana prestige
manu bird
marae courtyard
maunga mountain

moana sea or lake
moko tattoo
motu island, or anything that is isolated
pa fortified village
Pakeha foreigner, white person, European
po night
puke hill
puna spring (of water)
rangi sky
roto lake
rua two, eg Rotorua two lakes
tapu sacred
utu retribution
wai water
whanga bay, stretch of water, inlet
whare house
whenua land

'KIWI' ENGLISH

Aussie Australian
bach a holiday chalet (pronounced 'batch')
Beehive the main government building in Wellington
bludge scrounge, borrow
bush the forest
chook chicken
cocky farmer (usually cow-cocky)
chilly-bin portable cooler box
crib the South Island equivalent of a bach
crook sick, ill
dag a character, or entertaining person
dairy general store

gidday good day (hello)
good as gold fine, okay
handle beer glass with a handle
jandals flip-flops, thongs
judder bars bumps in the road to encourage motorists to drive slowly
morning tea mid-morning tea or coffee break
mozzie mosquito
Pakeha person of European descent
Pom an English person (mildly derogatory)
smoko tea or coffee break
togs swimwear
wopwops the back of beyond

Best places to see

1 Fiordland National Park

www.fiordland.org.nz

Fiordland National Park is not only the largest national park in New Zealand, but one of the largest in the world.

In contrast to the coast at the north of the South Island, where the Marlborough Sounds offer a gentle landscape of bush-clad hills and meandering sea passages, the sounds of Fiordland National Park in the south are rugged, glacier-carved fjords with deep waters and precipitous sides. Inland is an unspoiled region of hills, deep lakes and mountains covering 12,500sq km (4,800sq miles), where rare species of wildlife have survived undisturbed. The high annual rainfall produces dramatic waterfalls. The most northerly of the fjords is Milford Sound, and the road leading there is one of the scenic highlights of New Zealand. You can also fly to Milford, or walk the Milford Track (➤ 174) over four days. Most of the other fjords are inaccessible other than by sea. A boat trip on Milford Sound is recommended; tours last two hours to two days. Sheer cliffs rising 1,200m (4,000ft) out of the water provide awesome photographic opportunities, while some tours include a visit to Milford Deep Underwater Observatory for a glimpse of the unique ecology of the fjords. The trip to Doubtful Sound via Lake Manapouri (➤ 170) and the Wilmot Pass is also a must. Cruises of up to a week can be taken to some of the sounds. The gateway to Fiordland National Park is the township of Te Anau (➤ 175), on the shores of Lake Te Anau.

➕ 1X ✉ Access to Milford Sound via SH94, north of Te Anau
🕐 Snow chains may be required in winter ✋ Free access
🍴 Blue Duck Café and Bar ($$), Milford Sound (☎ 03 249 7931) 🚌 Tours from Te Anau and Queenstown; www.realjourneys.co.nz; www.redboats.co.nz 🚢 Milford Sound: daily launches ✈ Flights from Queenstown, Wanaka and Te Anau
ℹ Lakefront Drive, Te Anau ☎ 03 249 8900; Fiordland National Park Visitor Centre, Lakefront Drive, Te Anau ☎ 03 249 7924; www.doc.gov.nz

2 Tongariro National Park

This sacred 'land of fire', given by Maori to the New Zealand people in 1887, is now a UNESCO World Heritage Area.

Lying at the middle of the North Island's volcanic plateau is the island's highest mountain – the active volcanic peak of Mount Ruapehu (2,797m/9,176ft). Adjacent to it are Mount Ngauruhoe (2,291m/7,516 ft) and Mount Tongariro (1,968m/6,457ft), the trio forming the heart of a high and sometimes bleak area known as Tongariro National Park. The land was given to the government by the Maori tribal owners in 1887, when it became New Zealand's first – and the world's fourth – national park.

Tongariro is now North Island's most popular national park, mainly because of its excellent ski areas. The Whakapapa ski field lies on the northern slopes of Mount Ruapehu (20km/12 miles from the small community of National Park), and the Turoa field is on the southwestern slopes (served by the town of Ohakune). The ski season generally runs from about late June to September – although sometimes it can run even longer.

Ruapehu is an active volcano with a warm crater lake and, although normally placid, there were eruptions in 1995, 1996 and 2007 and it is monitored constantly.

Cone-shaped Ngauruhoe periodically emits a cloud of steam, but rarely erupts. Tongariro is dormant, but has a hot spring on its slopes.

There are pleasant walking trails through the park, including the Tongariro Alpine Crossing, a full-day trek across the shoulders of Mount Tongariro. From the track, it is possible to make a side trip to the top of Tongariro, or even to Ngauruhoe.

✚ 9H ✉ Whakapapa is at the end of SH48, off SH47 between SH1 and SH4 🕓 All year (roads may close due to winter snow) ✋ Free access 🍽 Chateau Tongariro ($$–$$$) at Whakapapa 🚌 National Park Ohakune and Whakapapa 🚆 National Park and Ohakune stations 🛈 Whakapapa Village, Mount Ruapehu ☎ 07 892 3729; www.mtruapehu.com

3 Museum of New Zealand Te Papa Tongarewa

www.tepapa.govt.nz

Bold, imaginative, constantly changing and always fun, Te Papa is New Zealand's leading-edge national museum.

Te Papa is a bicultural museum and has a variety of exhibitions that tell the stories, and display the *taonga* (treasures), of the Maori people, the *tangata whenua*, or first settlers of New Zealand.

Hands-on exhibitions such as Awesome Forces, Mountains to Sea and Blood, Earth, Fire describe the formation of the land, and the creatures that live on it, while Bush City brings the natural world into the middle of the capital. Passports dramatically conveys the stories of New Zealand's non-Maori immigrants, while Golden Days focuses on New Zealand life and culture through the medium of walk-in theatre. Toi Te Papa, covering nine galleries, contains 300 artworks dating from prehistory to the modern day. Te Papa's most recent exhibit, Our Space, is also its most innovative, with a range of interactive multimedia experiences and two action-packed rides.

For children there are Discovery Centres, with plenty of touchy-feely activities, plus StoryPlace for the very young.

✚ *Wellington 4e* ✉ Cable Street, Wellington ☎ 04 381 7000 🕐 Fri–Wed 10–6, Thu 10–9 ✋ General admission to Te Papa and most exhibitions free; charges (inexpensive) for some special exhibitions, Time Warp and guided tours 🍴 Te Papa Café ($); Espresso café ($)

4 Whakarewarewa Thermal Reserve

If you have time to see only one attraction in the Rotorua region, then 'Whaka' (as the reserve is commonly known) should be it.

The city of Rotorua (➤ 90), near the middle of the North Island, is renowned for volcanic activity, evidenced by spouting geysers, bubbling mud and a pervasive smell of hydrogen sulphide.

About 3km (2 miles) from the heart of the city, Whakarewarewa is the most famous of Rotorua's five thermal areas. The reserve is split into two areas. The main one, **Te Puia,** contains the Pohutu (Maori for 'splashing') geyser, which spouts up 30m (100ft) at regular intervals, and the smaller Prince of Wales Feathers geyser (12m/40ft), just to the north. Nearby are cauldrons of bubbling mud and moonscape-like silica formations.

Te Puia is also home to the New Zealand Maori Arts and Crafts Institute, established in the 1960s. There's also a shop and kiwi house, a concert of Maori songs and dance daily at 10:15, 12:15 and 3:15, and Te Po, an evening cultural

and dining experience, daily at 6:15.

The rest of the thermal reserve is taken up by **Whakarewarewa Thermal Village,** a living Maori village whose occupants escort tours, perform cultural shows and dish up *hangi* meals. Note that there is no access from here to the geysers.

✚ 10G

Te Puia

✉ Hemo Road, Rotorua ☎ 07 348 9047; www.tepuia.com ⏰ Oct–Mar daily 8–6; Apr–Sep 8–5 ✋ Expensive; guided tours depart on the hour every hour summer 9–5; winter 9–4
🍴 Maori meal (part of evening cultural tour)
🚌 Minibus transfers from Rotorua visitor centre

Whakarewarewa Thermal Village

✉ Tukiterangi Street, Rotorua ☎ 07 349 3463; www.whakarewarewa.com ⏰ Daily 8:30–5 (last admission 4:15) ✋ Moderate; includes cultural performances at 11:15, 2
🍴 *Hangi* daily 12–2

5 Abel Tasman National Park

Near the top of the South Island, this is neither New Zealand's largest nor grandest national park, but it remains one of the most popular.

The park is named after the first known European to see New Zealand, and its coastal location offers a stunning combination of native bush and golden-sand beaches. Access is via Kaiteriteri and Marahau to the south, and Wainui and Totaranui to the north. Road access within the park is limited – explore instead on foot or by sea kayak.

The easy and popular Coastal Track is one of the most beautiful in the country and takes three to four days to walk. Be sure to plan and watch out for tides if cutting across the lagoons. There are Department of Conservation huts and camp sites for overnight stays; passes should be purchased beforehand. Launches and water taxis also serve the bays so walkers can tackle short sections.

Like the Coastal Track, the Inland Track starts at Marahau and ends at Wainui, and takes around four days to complete. It crosses a more rugged landscape of peaks and forests, and has fine views to the bays and beaches below. A 45-minute detour leads to

Harwoods Hole, a limestone sinkhole that at 176m (577ft) is the deepest vertical shaft in New Zealand.

A popular alternative to walking the park's tracks is exploring its spectacular bays and headlands by kayak. Guided tours range from gentle half-day options to more strenuous three-day paddling and camping expeditions. Groups of two or more confident kayakers can also go it alone.

✚ 4P ✉ Northwest of Nelson, via SH60
☎ Abel Tasman Track hut reservations: 03 546 8210; www.doc.govt.nz 🕐 All year ✋ Free access; fee for huts and camp sites ($) 🍴 Awaroa Lodge ($$$); no road access; www.awaroalodge.co.nz 🚌 Daily tour buses from Nelson and Picton to Marahau, Kaiteriteri and Totaranui 🛥 Boat services daily from Totaranui, Kaiteriteri and Marahau ❓ Reduced transport facilities in winter ℹ Millers Acre, Nelson ☎ 03 546 939

6 Cape Reinga

A lighthouse at Cape Reinga, New Zealand's northernmost accessible point, guards the merging waters of the Tasman Sea and the Pacific Ocean.

From the promontory there are views of the coast, which sweeps away in a combination of cliffs and sand dunes. This is the departure point for Maori spirits returning to their legendary home of 'Hawaiki'.

Part of the thrill of a visit to Cape Reinga is the journey there. It's 121km (75 miles) north of Kaitaia and 225km (140 miles) beyond Paihia, from where most buses depart. You can drive, but one-day bus tours are popular as they include stops at a kauri forest and some include a 60km (37-mile) stretch along the misnamed Ninety Mile Beach on the western side of the peninsula. Rental vehicles are forbidden on this beach.

Access at the northern end is via a stream-bed with quicksand, and buses are the only vehicles allowed to cross. Nearby are giant sand dunes, which more adventurous visitors can surf down on boogie boards. There are few facilities here to detract from the spectacular setting, but there are more amenities are 23km (14 miles) south at Waitiki Landing.

✚ 9A ✉ Northern tip of the North Island, via SH1 ✋ Free access ❌ At Waitiki Landing ($$) 🚌 Daily tours from Kaitaia, Paihia, Kerikeri and Mangonui

ℹ Jaycee Park, South Road, Kaitaia ☎ 09 408 0879; www.visitnorthland.co.nz

7 Queenstown's Skyline Gondola

www.skyline.co.nz

One of the highlights of the South Island's premier tourist area is a ride high above the town on the Skyline Gondola.

The many attractions of Queenstown and its surrounding area are featured later in the book (➤ 158), but a great starting point for a visit is to take a ride on the Skyline Gondola cableway, which opened in 1967. The commanding view from the hilltop makes this a good way to get your bearings.

The ride itself, lasting just four minutes, takes visitors 450m (1,500ft) up the steep flank of Bob's Peak in small gondolas suspended from overhead cables. From the viewing platform at the top, the breathtaking scenes encompass Queenstown, Lake Wakatipu and the mountains of the Remarkables range.

The complex at the upper terminal houses a restaurant,

café and bar, and in the evenings Kiwi Haka, a cultural show, is staged. You can also do a bungee jump or tandem paraglide here, or take a chairlift ride above the complex and shoot back down along an 800m (875yd) track in a three-wheeled luge.

✚ 2W ✉ Brecon Street, Queenstown ☎ 03 441 0101 🕐 Gondola: daily 9–late; Kiwi Haka: daily 5:15, 6, 7:15, 8; luge: daily 10–30 minutes before dusk ✋ Gondola: moderate; Kiwi Haka: expensive; luge: inexpensive; bungy: expensive; paraglide: expensive 🍴 Café ($), restaurant ($$) and bar

8 The TranzAlpine

www.tranzalpine.co.nz

Crossing the Southern Alps via mountain passes, tunnels and viaducts, this single-track line links the east and west coasts of the South Island.

A success story of the recently nationalized rail system in New Zealand has been the promotion of the scenic route from Christchurch, through the Southern Alps, to the West Coast town of Greymouth. The TranzAlpine has become a popular tourist service, as a one-way link between the coasts, and as a round-trip excursion from Christchurch. The narrow-gauge train is diesel-hauled and the carriages have large picture windows; there is also a carriage with open sides for viewing and photography.

Departing daily from Christchurch in the morning, the train crosses the farmlands of the Canterbury Plains, passing through a number of small towns before stopping at Springfield. From here the journey is spectacular, as the train continues over viaducts and through tunnels across the Canterbury foothills up to Arthur's Pass. At 737m (2,417ft), this is the highest railroad station in the South Island and sees the arrival of many visitors bound for Arthur's Pass National Park, which offers numerous opportunities for hiking and mountaineering.

Shortly after leaving here, the train enters the 8km (5-mile) Otira Tunnel for the descent to Otira. On this side of the Southern Alps, the rainforests and scrubby landscapes of Westland offer a contrast to the eastern side. The line continues past mountains and along valleys before running beside the Grey River into Greymouth. The train returns to Christchurch in the afternoon.

✚ 3R–5S ✉ Christchurch station, Troup Drive, Addington ☎ 04 495 0775 🕓 Departs Christchurch daily 8:15am, return arrival 6:05pm 👆 Expensive 🍴 Refreshments available on train ($) 🚉 Christchurch; Greymouth

9 Aoraki/Mount Cook National Park

www.mtcooknz.com

New Zealand's highest peak, Aoraki/Mount Cook, forms the centrepiece of this beautiful alpine area in the heart of the South Island.

Much of the South Island is mountainous and the Southern Alps mountain range forms a backbone for most of the island's length. Of some 220 named peaks above 2,300m (7,500ft) in New Zealand, the highest, at 3,754m (12,313ft), commemorates both a Maori god and the English navigator who first landed in New Zealand in 1769. Nearby Mount Tasman is the second-highest peak, at 3,498m (11,473ft).

Aoraki/Mount Cook lies in the Aoraki/Mount Cook National Park, adjacent to Westland National Park. These two parks, together with Mount Aspiring (➤ 176) and Fiordland (➤ 36–37) national parks, have been incorporated into a UNESCO World Heritage Area.

Most of the alpine terrain of Aoraki/Mount Cook National Park is popular with trekkers and climbers. These mountains – 19 of them exceeding 3,000m (9,800ft) – offer a spectacular panorama of peaks, glaciers and rivers from trails of varying difficulty. Flights in

ski-equipped light aircraft are popular, taking in views of Aoraki/Mount Cook and the Alps, and include a landing on the snowfield of the Tasman Glacier – one of the longest glaciers in the world's temperate zones at 27km (17 miles).

Most coach tours include Mount Cook Village (dominated by the Hermitage Hotel), either looping in as a day trip, or staying a night or two.

✚ 3T ✉ At the end of SH80, 333km (206 miles) west of Christchurch
✋ Free access 🍴 Hermitage Hotel, Mount Cook Village ($$–$$$) 🚌 Buses from Christchurch and Queenstown
ℹ 1 Larch Grove, Aoraki/Mount Cook
☎ 03 435 1186

10 Waitomo Caves

www.waitomoinfo.co.nz

These are among New Zealand's most impressive natural wonders. Glow-worms twinkle like stars on the roof of a cave above an underground river.

The caves are some 200km (120 miles) south of Auckland, at the end of SH37 between the towns of Otorohanga and Te Kuiti. In the area are a number of rocky outcrops, with a labyrinth of caves and channels beneath. The two main caves open to the public are the Waitomo Glowworm Caves and the Aranui Cave. The former, which have given their name to the area, are the more popular. Visitors in guided parties are led through subterranean chambers of varying sizes containing delicate limestone stalactite and stalagmite formations highlighted by special lighting effects.

The main attraction of the Waitomo Glowworm Caves, however, is the boat ride along an underground stream into a cave where you can gaze up at thousands of glow-worms lighting up the roof like stars. The effect is created by the 'lights' that the tiny insect larvae create to lure prey into their mesh of sticky mucus threads.

The Aranui Cave is worth visiting for its beautiful limestone formations, although it does not have the bonus of glow-worms. The quieter Ruakuri Cave has glow-worms as well as an underground river; this is the scene of many black-water rafting tours.

The caves are usually busy with coach tours in the middle of the day, so try to avoid this time. At the visitor centre, the Museum of Caves has good

audiovisual displays. Except for a hotel, there are few facilities near the caves.

➕ 8G ✉ On SH37, 8km (5 miles) off SH3, south of Otorohanga ☎ 07 878 7640 🕐 26 Dec–Feb daily 8:45–7; Mar–Sep 8:45–5; Oct–24 Dec 8:45–5:30 💲 Expensive 🍴 Waitomo Caves Hotel ($$) 🚌 Minibus transfers from intercity buses 🚉 Transfers from Otorohanga station ❓ Included in most North Island coach tours

Best things to do

Great places to have lunch

Boat Shed Café ($$$)

The Boat Shed has a well-deserved reputation for its fresh seafood dishes and its views across the waters of Tasman Bay to the distant mountains beyond are simply breathtaking.

✉ 351 Wakefield Quay, Nelson ☎ 03 546 9783

Boulcott Street Bistro ($$$)

If you are seeking somewhere with a touch of class in the capital, look no further. The classic dishes here use fresh seasonal ingredients and are accompanied by a well thought-out wine list.

✉ 99 Boulcott Street, Wellington ☎ 04 499 4199

Cin Cin on Quay ($$$)

For more than 20 years this downtown waterfront restaurant has remained one of Auckland's favourites. The European-style dishes make use of New Zealand's best produce, served up in lively surroundings.

✉ 99 Quay Street, Auckland ☎ 09 307 6966

Dux de Lux ($$)

The relaxed Dux de Lux brewery restaurant has an eclectic menu with both indoor and outdoor seating. Its main drawcard, however, is its location.

✉ Corner of Hereford and Montreal streets, Christchurch
☎ 03 366 6919

Gibbston Valley Winery ($$)

Gibbston Valley was the first commercial vineyard in Central Otago when it was established in 1987. The restaurant here is the perfect place to enjoy a glass or two of the winery's world-class pinot noir, accompanied by mouth-watering Mediterranean-style dishes.

✉ Queenstown–Cromwell SH6 (24km/15miles from Queenstown)
☎ 03 442 6910

Iguaçu ($$)

Parnell is known for its trendy boutiques and cafés and Iguaçu has long been part of that scene, and continues to be popular for its Pacific Rim-style food.

✉ 269 Parnell Road, Auckland ☎ 09 358 4804

Matterhorn ($$–$$$)

First opened in 1963 by two Swiss brothers, this is still where the capital's cool crowd congregates. Take a break from shopping along trendy Cuba Street and chill out as you tuck into some of the innovative bistro food dished up here.

✉ 106 Cuba Street, Wellington ☎ 04 384 3359

Pegasus Bay ($$$)

Pegasus Bay is a beautiful spot for an alfresco lunch half an hour's drive north of Christchurch. The dishes are created with the wines in mind, and each comes with a recommendation.

✉ Stockgrove Road, Waipara ☎ 03 314 6869

Plato ($$)

Although Dunedin's top café is tucked away down by the harbourfront, it is well worth searching out. It is open for dinner daily, but the Sunday brunch/lunch is particularly popular, with everything from American pancakes to whole grilled crayfish.

✉ 2 Birch Street, Dunedin ☎ 03 477 4235

Portage Resort Hotel ($$$)

The location of the Portage Resort is reason enough to make the trip out here from Picton. Soak up the divine views as you dine in style in the restaurant, or opt for something lighter in the more casual waterfront café.

✉ Kenepuru Sound, Picton ☎ 03 573 4309

Top activities

Bird-watching: From October through to March, take a tour to see white herons roost near Whataroa in Westland.

Four-wheel-drive safari: Follow an old stage-coach road on the Dunstan Trail, out of Alexandra.

Golfing: There are more than 400 courses in the country!

Just looking: Kelly Tarlton's Antarctic Encounter and Underwater World, in Auckland.

Maori experience: Visit a *marae* or eat a *hangi*.

Skiing: Try Coronet Peak, near Queenstown.

Swimming: Brilliant beaches, rivers and lakes everywhere.

Trout fishing: Open season year-round at Taupo.

Walking: From Arataki Visitor Centre in Auckland's Waitakere Ranges to experience the New Zealand bush.

Wine trail: Tour the splendid Marlborough vineyards.

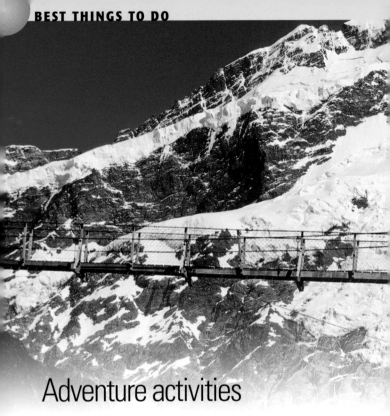

Adventure activities

New Zealand offers a wide variety of popular adventure and thrill activities, such as jet-boating, bungee jumping, paragliding and white-water rafting. While Queenstown is the home for many of these activities, they are also available elsewhere.

The South Island's Southern Alps mountain chain offers many climbing and mountaineering opportunities for varying skill levels.

Big-game fishing: Bay of Islands (➤ 86).

Bungee jumping: Queenstown (➤ 158–160).

Canoeing: Whanganui River (➤ 109).

Glacier walking: Fox Glacier (➤ 169).

Hang-gliding: Around Queenstown (➤ 158–160).

Horseback riding: Old gold-mining trails around Cromwell (➤ 164).

Jet-boating: Queenstown's Shotover River jet-boat (➤ 161).

White-water rafting: Try the Kaituna River near Rotorua (➤ 90) or Skippers Canyon (➤ 161).

Wilderness walking: The Heaphy Track (➤ 146) or Milford Track (➤ 174).

a walk around Wellington

An extra dimension is given to this walk by first taking a breathtaking ride on the Cable Car (➤ 111) from its terminus in Cable Car Lane, off Lambton Quay, up past Victoria University to the Kelburn terminus. From here on it's all downhill.

After alighting from the Cable Car, go to the lookout points to admire the city and harbour views that spread out before you.

Immediately adjacent is the upper entrance to the Botanic Garden (➤ 111). Follow any of the paths downhill through native bush to the Lady Norwood Rose Garden.

At the bottom, continue around Anderson Park then go through Bolton Street Memorial Park. Continue over the highway and after that walk down to Bowen Street.

Stroll through the grounds of Parliament, passing the Beehive, Parliament House and the Parliamentary Library buildings. Exit onto Molesworth Street and cross over to the National Library, which includes the Alexander Turnbull Library (➤ 112).

Continue walking up Molesworth Street, then turn right onto Pipitea Street to reach Mulgrave Street.

Here you can take the opportunity to visit Old St Paul's Church (➤ 112), and admire its interior design and decoration.

Continue down Mulgrave Street and past the railway station to reach Queens Wharf. Reward yourself with a coffee or glass of wine at one of the waterfront cafés here before returning to Cable Car Lane.

Distance 2.5km (1.5 miles)
Time 1.5 hours plus stops
Start/end point Cable Car Lane, off Lambton Quay ✚ *Wellington 3d*
Lunch Café Littera ($) ✉ National Library, corner of Molesworth and Aitken streets ☎ 04 474 3000 🕓 Mon–Fri 8–4

Places to take the children

AUCKLAND
Auckland Zoo
Popular with children, especially for elephants, lions and hippos (➤ 76).

Sky Tower
Over-10s can brave the Sky Walk or Sky Jump (➤ 81).

CHRISTCHURCH
International Antarctic Centre
Penguins, rides and polar experiences (➤ 142).

Orana Wildlife Park
African and native animals in natural settings (➤ 142).

Science Alive!
Hands-on displays in the former railway station (➤ 137).

NAPIER
National Aquarium of New Zealand
Displays of native and exotic species (➤ 121).

QUEENSTOWN
Skyline Gondola
Take the cablecar up above the city (➤ 48–49).

ROTORUA
Agrodome
Don't miss milking a cow at this farm and activities complex (➤ 91).

WANAKA
Puzzling World
A modern maze and eccentric or puzzling attractions (➤ 176).

WELLINGTON
Carter Observatory and Planetarium
The observatory is in the Botanic Garden, near the top terminal of the Cable Car, and has a multimedia experience, planetarium shows and telescope-viewing sessions (► 111).

Stunning views

Akaroa Harbour from Hilltop on SH75 (➤ 145): Superb views on the road that joins Christchurch with the Banks Peninsula (➤ 144).

Aoraki/Mount Cook (➤ 52) **and Mount Tasman, reflected in the waters of Lake Matheson, near Fox Glacier** (➤ 169): The best time to go is on a clear day.

Auckland city from the Sky Tower (➤ 81): Stand on the observation deck's clear floor for views down as well as out.

Cape Reinga (➤ 46): Imagine the Maori spirits of the dead leaping off from this point to return to their ancestral homeland, 'Hawaiki'.

Hawke's Bay from Te Mata Peak (► 121): Drive to the top of this 399m (1,300ft) summit for a 360-degree panorama.

Mitre Peak from a Milford Sound cruise boat (► 36): This pyramidal peak is one of the iconic images of New Zealand.

Wellington city from the Cable Car (► 111): Look out over the capital and its harbour, then take a leisurely stroll through the Botanic Gardens.

Whale tail, Kaikoura, from a whale-watching boat (► 146): View a whale's tail with the Kaikoura Ranges in the background.

Exploring

New Zealand is in the South Pacific, 2,000km (1,200 miles) from Australia and at the opposite end of the world as far as many visitors are concerned. Today the country's remoteness, pristine environment and lack of crowds have made it particularly attractive to tourists. Combine this with modern communications and transport networks, and it's easy to see why tourist numbers have shot up.

Visitors who arrive on New Zealand's shores will not be disappointed, for this is a country that packs a lot into its relatively small area. North Island, the smaller of the two main islands, has historic sights to visit, volcanoes and geysers, and a vibrant Maori cultural scene. It is also home to Auckland and Wellington, the two largest cities. The South Island, meanwhile, is renowned for its dramatic mountain scenery, wilderness areas and unique flora and fauna.

Upper North Island

This quarter of New Zealand, which includes the largest city, Auckland, is home to more than half the country's population. In 1840, New Zealand's founding document, the Treaty of Waitangi, was signed by Maori chiefs and representatives of the British Crown in the Bay of Islands. Near the northern tip of Northland is Cape Reinga, where Maori spirits of the deceased are said to depart for their ancient Polynesian home.

Auckland

One hour's drive east of Auckland is the Coromandel Peninsula, a beautiful but rugged area of forest trails, old gold mines, deserted beaches and arts and crafts outlets. There's plenty on offer to suit everyone and a range of activities and sights.

About three hours' drive southeast of Auckland is Rotorua, the heart of traditional Maori culture in a geothermally active region of lakes, forests and volcanic remnants.

Farther south, in the middle of the North Island, is the resort town of Taupo, which can be found nestling on the shore of Lake Taupo with a distant view of the brooding volcanoes of magnificent Tongariro National Park.

AUCKLAND

The city, built over the remnants of 48 volcanoes, sprawls across a narrow isthmus between the Pacific Ocean and the Tasman Sea. With a population of 1.3 million, it is New Zealand's largest and most cosmopolitan city as well as being the main commercial and industrial base. Auckland also offers an array of cultural and sporting activities. Auckland is the major New Zealand gateway for air and sea passengers, and there are road, rail and long-distance bus services to most parts of the North Island.

European settlement began here in 1840, and it was New Zealand's capital until 1865. The compact downtown area is still its hub, but there are major shopping and entertainment areas beyond the central streets, and the attractions for visitors spread to and beyond the suburbs.

www.aucklandnz.com

✚ 8E

🛈 SKYCITY Hotel, corner of Victoria and Federal streets ☎ 09 367 6009

Albert Park

Conveniently situated close to downtown Auckland, this formal garden has a Victorian pavilion and statuary among its many flowerbeds and trees, just waiting to be discovered.

Unsurprisingly, it is well used as a shady retreat by city office workers and students from the Auckland University campus looking for a little rest and relaxation.

✚ *Auckland 5c* ✉ Princes Street ☎ 09 379 2020 🅘 Unrestricted
✋ Free access

Aotea Square
This central city square is the focus of Auckland's performing arts scene. Managed by THE EDGE, the venues here include the square itself, used as a setting for open-air concerts; the Aotea Centre, home to a concert hall, theatre, exhibition areas, restaurants and bars; and the Auckland Town Hall (1911) and stunning Civic Theatre (1929), both of which now also host concert performances.

✚ *Auckland 4c* ✉ Queen Street ☎ 09 357 3355; www.the-edge.co.nz
🅘 Box office: Mon–Fri 9–5:30, Sat–Sun 10–4

Auckland Art Gallery

Located within a Victorian edifice, the main gallery displays a prominent collection of New Zealand and overseas paintings, prints and drawings. Important touring exhibitions from overseas are also shown here (admission charge). The main gallery is closed for renovation until 2011; in the meantime, exhibitions and events are housed in the New Gallery, opposite. Nearby is the Auckland Central Public Library, with historic and rare books.

www.aucklandartgallery.govt.nz

✚ *Auckland 5c* ✉ Corner of Wellesley and Kitchener streets ☎ 09 379 1349 🕐 Daily 10–5 👋 Free; special exhibitions inexpensive 🍴 Reuben ($$) ❓ Free guided tour 2pm

Auckland Zoo

Near the Museum of Transport and Technology (➤ 80), and connected to it by vintage tram, Auckland's zoo houses the usual overseas creatures plus native species such as the kiwi and other endemic birds. There's a farm animal section for children and Pridelands, a simulated African savannah enclosure with giraffes, zebras and other animals. The zoo's endangered species programme is internationally recognized.

www.aucklandzoo.co.nz

✚ *Auckland 1f (off map)* ✉ Motions Road, Western Springs ☎ 09 360 3805 🕐 Sep–May daily 9:30–5:30; Jun–Aug 9.30–5; last admission 4:15 👋 Moderate 🍴 Café and kiosks ($) 🚌 045

Devonport

Ten minutes across the harbour, the attractive North Shore suburb of Devonport has many 19th-century buildings housing cafés, bookshops, craft galleries, antiques shops and a couple of museums.

✚ *Auckland 7a (off map)* ⛴ Ferries from Quay Street: Fullers ☎ 09 367 9111; www.fullers.co.nz, www.devonport.co.nz ℹ 3 Victoria Road, Devonport ☎ 09 446 0677

The Domain and Auckland Museum

The Domain's 75ha (185 acres) of parkland lie between downtown and Newmarket. The Wintergardens display exotic plants in a hot-house and there is also a dell of New Zealand ferns. In the Domain, the impressive Auckland Museum houses extensive collections of Maori and Polynesian objects, the flora and fauna of New Zealand, arts and crafts from other countries, and a war memorial display. The museum often hosts special exhibitions.

✛ Domain: *Auckland 6d;* Museum: *Auckland 6e* ✉ Museum: Auckland Domain, Parnell ☎ 09 306 7067 (infoline); www.aucklandmuseum.com
🕐 Daily 10–5 🍴 Columbus Café ($) 🖐 Donation; charge for exhibitions and concerts ❓ Maori concerts ($$) 11, 12, 1:30 daily, plus 2:30 in summer

Harbour Bridge
Arching across Waitemata Harbour (► 83) to the North Shore suburbs, the bridge is more than 1km (0.5 miles) long. It opened in 1959 with four lanes, later widened to eight. Harbour cruises go under it and sightseeing buses go over it, but there's no access for pedestrians – except for bridge-climbers and bungee jumpers.

🏢 *Auckland 1a (off map)* ☎ 09 361 2000 (Auckland Bridge Climb and Bungy); www.bungy.co.nz ⏱ Trips daily at 9, 11:30, 2:30. Closed public holidays
💲 Expensive ❓ Views of the bridge from Shelly Beach Road and Westhaven Drive; beware of one-way streets

Kelly Tarlton's Antarctic Encounter and Underwater World

This aquarium has walk-through transparent acrylic tunnels and more than 2,000 fish and other marine animals, including sharks from the waters around New Zealand. Next door is Stingray Bay, home to Phoebe, a 2m (6.5ft) stingray.

There is also a ride through a re-creation of an Antarctic landscape, with a replica of explorer Captain Scott's 1911 hut and a colony of penguins.

www.kellytarltons.co.nz

✚ *Auckland 8c (off map)*

✉ 23 Tamaki Drive, Orakei ☎ 09 531 5065 🕐 Daily 9–6 (last admission 5) 👋 Moderate 🍽 Refreshment Kiosk ($) 🚌 Free shuttle daily on the hour 9–4 from SKYCITY Hotel Atrium

Mount Eden and One Tree Hill

Respectively the highest (196m/643ft) and second highest (183m/600ft) of Auckland's mainland volcanic peaks, both provide panoramic views. Roads go to the top of both, but most sightseeing tours opt for Mount Eden. Both were former Maori *pa* (fortresses), and terracing and storage pits are still visible.

🚹 *Auckland 4f (off map)* ✉ Mount Eden: access off Hillside Crescent, Mount Eden Road; One Tree Hill: access off Manukau Road at Royal Oak
🌐 Unrestricted access

Museum of Transport and Technology

This museum, spread over two sites, displays vintage cars, aircraft, trams, colonial buildings and other technological items

from yesteryear, largely maintained by volunteer groups. Exhibits include a replica of Richard Pearse's aircraft, which reputedly flew near Timaru earlier than the Wright brothers' more famous flight; and the only Solent Mark IV flying boat left in the world. Admission includes a return ride to Auckland Zoo (➤ 76) on a historic tram.

www.motat.org.nz

✚ *Auckland 1f (off map)* ✉ 805 Great North Road, Western Springs
☎ 09 815 5800 🕓 Daily 10–5 ✋ Moderate 🍴 Café ($) 🚌 045

New Zealand National Maritime Museum

New Zealand has a considerable maritime heritage, and this is explored inside old warehouses next to the waterfront. Displays cover Polynesian exploration, European immigration, shipwrecks and

lighthouses, and there is a tribute to America's Cup yachtsman Sir Peter Blake. Harbour trips in heritage vessels are regular events.

www.maritimemuseum.co.nz

✚ *Auckland 4b* ✉ Corner of Quay and Hobson streets ☎ 09 373 0800
🕓 Daily 9–5 ✋ Moderate 🍴 Waterfront Café ($$)

Sky Tower

The tallest structure in the southern hemisphere at 328m (1,076ft) the tower has three observation decks, two restaurants and a bar, and a glass floorplate. Those with a head for heights can try the 192m (630ft) Sky Jump bungee or the Sky Walk.

www.skycityauckland.co.nz

✚ *Auckland 4c* ✉ Corner of Victoria and Federal streets ☎ 09 363 6000
🕓 Sun–Thu 8:30am–10:30pm, Fri–Sat 8:30am–11:30pm ✋ Moderate
🍴 Sky Lounge Café ($$), Observatory and Orbit ($$$) restaurants

Around Auckland

AUCKLAND BOTANIC GARDENS

These 64ha (158 acre) gardens south of the city house some 10,000 exotic and native plants. If your time is limited, visit Eden Garden instead, on the eastern flank of Mount Eden (➤ 80).

www.auincklandbotanicgardens.co.nz

✚ 8E ✉ 102 Hill Road, Manurewa; south of Auckland ☎ 09 267 1457 ◷ Daily 8–dusk ▨ Free ▮ Café ($$)

WAITAKERE RANGES

A picturesque route, with bush scenery and views across the city, winds through the forested hills to Auckland's west. Signposted as Scenic Drive, it starts at Titirangi and passes through native

bush to **Arataki Visitor Centre,** where cantilevered platforms provide breathtaking views of the rainforest and Manukau Harbour. The centre has displays about the wildlife and plants of the area, and leaflets describing local nature walks. You can also drive on to the beautiful ocean beaches of Piha, Karekare, Bethells (Te Henga) and Muriwai, where you can see a gannet colony close up.

8E

Arataki Visitor Centre

☎ 09 817 0077; www.arc.govt.nz ⊙ Oct–Apr daily 9–5; May–Sep Mon–Fri 10–4, Sat–Sun 9–5 ✋ Free

WAITEMATA HARBOUR AND HAURAKI GULF

Waitemata Harbour, on the northern side of the isthmus, opens onto the Hauraki Gulf. You can explore both by fast and frequent catamarans, ferries, launches and yachts from the Ferry Terminal on Quay Street.

The most popular of the Hauraki Gulf islands is Waiheke, 40 minutes from Auckland by fast ferry. Craft shops, vineyards and superb beaches are among its numerous attractions.

The volcanic cone of Rangitoto is the nearest island to the city. The last eruption that occurred here is thought to have taken place sometime within the past 600 years. You can take a safari tour to just below the summit, or you can walk to the crater in about one hour.

Auckland 7a 🚢 Regular ferries, boat tours and Rangitoto tour: Fullers ☎ 09 367 9111; www.fullers.co.nz ✋ Cruise prices vary 🍴 Cin Cin on Quay ($$$; ➤ 58) and Mudbrick Restaurant ($$$) on Waiheke Island (➤ 100)

a drive through suburban Auckland

Starting from the Ferry Building on Quay Street, this drive heads east around the bays of Tamaki Drive to St Heliers, then loops inland to the suburbs of Remuera and Newmarket before returning via Parnell to Quay Street.

Tamaki Drive passes the public Parnell Swimming Baths and Okahu Bay. Kelly Tarlton's Antarctic Encounter and Underwater World (➤ 79) is a worthwhile stop.

Continue to Mission Bay, a popular swimming beach and an area of busy cafés. A short walk to the Bastion Point headland provides vistas of the harbour and Hauraki Gulf (➤ 83). Drive on to Kohimarama and the waterfront village of St Heliers.

Turn right onto St Heliers Bay Road. Follow this up the hill to the St Johns Road traffic lights, where you turn left onto St Johns Road, then right at the traffic circle.

This leads to Remuera Road and through the wealthy suburb of Remuera, to the fashionable entertainment and shopping area of Newmarket. Turn right on Broadway and continue straight on to Parnell Road. Domain Drive on your left leads to The Domain and Auckland Museum (➤ 77).

You could take a one-hour stroll down Parnell Road, parking if possible near the Holy Trinity Cathedral at the top of the road. The area around the colonial-style Parnell Village has many restaurants, cafés, craft shops and boutiques.

Continue driving, turning right just past the cathedral into St Stephens Avenue and left onto Gladstone Road. Pause at the Dove-Myer Robinson Park for a breather and a view of the harbour before returning to the Ferry Building.

Distance 24km (15 miles)
Time 1 hour plus stops; suggest at least half a day
Start/end point Ferry Building, Quay Street ✚ *Auckland 5b*
Lunch Iguaçu ($$; ➤ 59) ✉ 269 Parnell Road, Parnell
☎ 09 358 4804

More to see in the Upper North Island

BAY OF ISLANDS

In addition to being one of New Zealand's most historically interesting regions for both Europeans and Maori, this is among the North Island's most popular resort areas. The Bay of Islands Maritime and Historic Park consists of more than 800km (500 miles) of coastline and some 150 islands, as well as many reserves on the surrounding mainland and the communities of Paihia, Russell and Kerikeri.

➕ 8B

ℹ The Wharf, Marsden Road, Paihia ☎ 09 402 7345

Kerikeri

Kerikeri, 23km (14 miles) from Paihia, is known for its citrus-fruit orchards and craft workshops. Historic sites near the small harbour include the **Mission House,** erected in 1822 as the country's second mission station and now the oldest surviving building in New Zealand; and the **Stone Store** (1836), now a living museum selling old-fashioned goods, from seeds to blankets. Across the inlet is **Rewa's Village,** a reconstruction of a pre-European Maori fishing village, and well worth a visit.

➕ 7B
Mission House and Stone Store
✉ Kerikeri Basin ☎ 09 407 9236
🕐 Nov–Apr daily 10–5; May–Oct
10–4 ✋ Inexpensive
Rewa's Village
✉ Landing Road ☎ 09 407 6454
🕐 Nov–Apr daily 9–5; May–Oct 10–4
✋ Inexpensive

Paihia
Paihia sprawls over three bays.
Its town centre is the wharf, from
where various scenic and nature
cruises depart, as well as a
regular passenger service across
to Russell (➤ 88). Restaurants,
accommodation
and cafés are plentiful.

From the southern end of
Paihia, the Opua-Paihia Coastal
Walkway is an attractive 5.8km
(3.5-mile) walk – allow about
2–3 hours each way. The scenery
includes sandy beaches and
mangrove boardwalks. Adjacent
to the walkway is Harrison's
Bush Scenic Reserve, one of
the area's best examples of
coastal forest.
www.northlandnz.com
➕ 7B
ℹ The Wharf, Marsden Road
☎ 09 402 7345

Russell

Russell, New Zealand's first European settlement, was known as 'the hell-hole of the Pacific' back in the days when lawless whalers came into violent contact with local Maori and each other. The town is now a quiet hamlet, although the bullet holes in the 1836 wooden church and the graves in its churchyard testify to its lively past. Other sights include the 1842 **Pompallier,** built as part of the French Catholic mission, and nearby Flagstaff Hill – scene of disputes between British troops and local Maori in the 1840s. The **Russell Museum** has a one-fifth scale model of Cook's ship *Endeavour*.

✚ 8B

Pompallier

✉ The Strand ☎ 09 403 9015 🕓 Nov–Apr daily 10–5; May–Oct 10–4 ✋ Inexpensive

Russell Museum

✉ 2 York Street ☎ 09 403 7701 🕓 Feb–Dec daily 10–4; Jan 10–5 ✋ Inexpensive

Waitangi Historic Reserve

Just north of Paihia is the Waitangi Historic Reserve, where, in 1840, a treaty was signed by Maori chiefs and the British Crown under the auspices of Captain (later Governor) William Hobson. The treaty promised the Maori people rights in exchange for British sovereignty, but its interpretation remains controversial today. The Treaty House, built in 1834 for the British government official, is open to visitors. The Waitangi Treaty Grounds also display a centennial (1940) Maori meeting house and a 35m (115ft) Maori *waka* (war canoe), and there are cultural performances and tours.

www.waitangi.net.nz

✚ 7B ✉ Tau Henare Drive, near Paihia ☎ 09 402 7437 🕓 Oct–Apr daily 8:30am–9:30pm; May–Sep 9–5 ✋ Moderate 🍴 Waikokopu Café ($$)

COROMANDEL PENINSULA

A good place to start your Coromandel trip is Thames, a town with a gold-mining past that now acts as a gateway to the peninsula. From here SH25 meanders north up the west coast, over forested volcanic hills, to the town of Coromandel. This centre for arts and crafts also has a boating and fishing harbour.

Over on the east coast, don't miss stunning Cathedral Cove, which is great for snorkelling and diving, and Hot Water Beach, where you can dig your own private spa in the sand. Captain Cook anchored the *Endeavour* off nearby Cooks Beach in 1769 to observe the transit of the planet Mercury across the sun.

www.thecoromandel.com

✚ 9E

ℹ 206 Pollen Street, Thames ☎ 07 868 7284

NORTHLAND

In the subtropical far north of New Zealand you will find the country's longest beach, as well as its tallest trees – the impressive kauri at Waipoua Forest.

🚩 7C

Cape Reinga

Best places to see, ➤ 46–47.

Waipoua Forest

This forest is a remnant of the bush that once covered nearly all the Northland region. New Zealand kauri is one of the world's oldest-growing and largest trees, with a long, straight trunk up to 50m (160ft) tall. Its golden timber was highly prized, and its gum used to make lacquer. The scenic road through the reserve passes many of these trees; the largest, called Tane Mahuta, is reached via a short bush walk.

🚩 7C ✉ SH12; 112km (69 miles) from Paihia ☎ 09 439 3011; www.doc.govt.nz 🕓 Unrestricted 🖐 Free

ROTORUA

The city of Rotorua, 234km (145 miles) southeast of Auckland, is recognized as the North Island's leading tourist centre because of its Maori culture, scenic variety and geothermal activity. The latter becomes apparent in the form of sulphurous odours near the city. Whakarewarewa (➤ 42) is the city's leading geothermal reserve, but the area has a number of other places with such activity, plus a dozen lakes, an evergreen forest and a host of other attractions (➤ 90–95). The main shopping thoroughfare is Tutanekai Street.

www.rotoruanz.com
➕ 10G
🏠 1167 Fenton Street ☎ 07 348 5179

Agrodome

Here the story of sheep in the New Zealand economy is told with regular sheep-shearing displays, lamb feeding, mock sheep auctions, and sheep and cattle shows. Tours of the farm are available and you can buy woollen goods at the shop.
www.agrodome.co.nz
➕ 10F ✉ Western Road, Ngongotaha ☎ 07 357 1050 🕐 Daily 8:30–5; sheep shows 9:30, 11, 2:30; farm tours 10:40, 12:10, 1:30, 3:40 ✋ Moderate

Hell's Gate and the Waiy Ora Spa

The reserve here covers about 20ha (50 acres), and an extensive walk takes visitors past pools of hot water, bubbling mud and other features. Irish playwright George Bernard Shaw is supposed to have given the area its name on seeing it. The spa offers several thermal water and mud baths and treatments.

www.hellsgate.co.nz

✚ 10F ✉ SH30, Tikitere; 18km (11 miles) northeast of Rotorua ☎ 07 345 3151 🕑 Daily 8:30–8:30 ✋ Moderate; spa and treatments expensive

Lake Rotorua

This is the largest of a dozen or so lakes in the region, formed in a volcanic crater, and can be explored on a cruise or self-drive rental boat. Mokoia Island, in the middle of the lake, is the setting for a Maori legend about two young lovers, Hinemoa and Tutanekai.

www.rotoruanz.com

✚ 10F ℹ 1167 Fenton Street, Rotorua ☎ 07 348 5179

Ohinemutu

Ohinemutu, a Maori village on the shore of Lake Rotorua, was once the main settlement here. It is of interest for its Anglican **St Faith's Church** (notice the window showing Christ dressed in a Maori cloak), and a carved Maori meeting house (not open to the public).

St Faith's Church

✉ Mataiawhea Street 🕑 Daily 9–4
✋ Free; donations welcome
ℹ 1167 Fenton Street, Rotorua ☎ 07 348 5179

Rainbow Springs Nature Park

The natural freshwater springs welling up here on the side of Mount Ngongotaha are stocked with four species of trout that can be observed in the fern-fringed pools and fed with fish food. Also at the park are tuatara and several native birds, including kiwis in a specially designed enclosure. Night-time tours see the kiwis emerge into the open.

www.rainbowsprings.co.nz
✉ Fairy Springs Road
☎ 07 350 0440 🕐 Oct–May daily 8am–11pm; Jun–Sep 8am–10pm. Kiwi Encounter tours: daily 10–4 ✋ Expensive
🍽 Café ($)

Skyline Skyrides
Mount Ngongotaha (757m/ 2,483ft) is a prominent peak on the western shore of Lake Rotorua. Although there is a road to the top, the Skyrides gondola is a popular attraction, taking passengers 180m (590ft) to a viewpoint halfway up the mountain, offering a panorama of the city and lake. At the top you can race part of the way back down on a three-wheel luge, returning to the top on a chairlift.
www.skylineskyrides.co.nz
✉ Fairy Springs Road
☎ 07 347 0027 🕐 Daily 9–late
✋ Gondola: moderate. Luge: inexpensive 🍽 Café ($$); restaurant ($$$)

Te Wairoa Buried Village

In 1886 the dormant volcano of Mount Tarawera erupted, resulting in loss of life and the destruction of several villages – including Te Wairoa – which was buried under ash and mud.

Also obliterated were the famous Pink and White Terraces, fan-like natural silica formations on the shores of Lake Rotomahana. The village of Te Wairoa has since been partly excavated, and may be seen separately or as part of a round-trip visit incorporating other sites.

Tours of the volcano can be arranged at Rotorua's visitor centre in Fenton Street.

www.buriedvillage.co.nz

✚ 10G ✉ Tarawera Road; 14km (8.5 miles) from Rotorua

☎ 07 362 8287 ◷ Nov–Mar daily 9–5; Apr–Oct 9–4:30

🚌 Shuttle from city available (027 494 5508; $$)

✋ Moderate 🍴 Café ($)

Waimangu Volcanic Valley

The 1886 Tarawera eruption that destroyed Te Wairoa also created the impressively active Waimangu Volcanic Valley and nearby Lake Rotomahana. There is a walk past thermal pools, including Frying Pan Lake, the world's largest hot-water spring, and a path leads down to Lake Rotomahana, where cruises sail past steaming cliffs and over the sunken site of the Pink and White Terraces (► above).

www.waimangu.com

🕂 10G ✉ Off SH5; 19km (11.5 miles) south of Rotorua ☎ 07 366 6137 ⏰ Feb–Dec daily 8:30–5 (last admission 3:45); Jan 8:30–6 (last admission 4:45) ✋ Expensive

Wai-O-Tapu Thermal Wonderland

The most colourful of the geothermal areas, Wai-O-Tapu encompasses thermal zones that have been given their different hues by mineral deposits. Highlights include the Lady Knox Geyser, which erupts every morning at 10:15, and can reach heights of 20m (65.5ft), and the hot Champagne Pool.

There are three different walks around the main park. Graphic displays provide basic information on volcanic activity, fauna and flora.

www.geyserland.co.nz

🕂 10G ✉ Off SH5; 27km (16.5 miles) south of Rotorua ☎ 07 366 6333 ⏰ Daily 8:30–5 (last admission 3:45) ✋ Moderate

Whakarewarewa Thermal Reserve

Best places to see, ➤ 42–43.

TAUPO

The town of Taupo nestles at the heart of the North Island beside Lake Taupo, looking out towards the distant peaks of the Tongariro National Park. Together with the surrounding area, it has become a major holiday destination and offers visitors a wealth of attractions.

www.laketauponz.com

✚ 9G ℹ️ Tongariro Street ☎ 07 376 0027

Huka Falls

Near Wairakei, where the Waikato River plunges over an 11m (36ft) drop, are the Huka Falls. The huge volume of water that crashes through this narrow defile makes it a thunderous spectacle. There are various vantage points along the path.

www.hukafalls.com

✚ 9G ✉️ Off SH1, 5km (3 miles) north of Taupo 🕐 Daily, open access
✋ Free

Huka Prawn Park

Tropical prawns are grown here using waste geothermal water from the adjacent power station. Take a tour, then catch some prawns and have them cooked in the restaurant.

www.hukaprawnpark.co.nz

✚ 10G ✉ Huka Falls Road ☎ 07 374 8474 ⚙ Nov–Apr daily 9–4:30; May–Oct 9:30–4:30 ✋ Moderate

Lake Taupo

Formed by two massive volcanic eruptions, 26,500 years ago and in AD186, Lake Taupo, covering 600sq km (232sq miles), is the largest lake in New Zealand. The lake is internationally renowned for its trout fishing; there are cruises available.

✚ 9H 🚢 Lake cruises depart from Taupo Boat Harbour

ℹ Tongariro Street, Taupo ☎ 07 376 0027

Waipahihi Botanical Gardens

This 34ha (85-acre) drive-through reserve has walks lined with native trees, and beds of stunning rhododendrons and azaleas.

✚ 10G ✉ Shepherd Road ☎ 07 378 9417 ⚙ Daily, open access ✋ Free

Wairakei Terraces

The Wairakei terraces are a man-made re-creation of the natural silica formations that existed before the development of the power station here in 1958. Also on site are evening cultural tours, based around a re-created Maori village.

www.wairakeiterraces.co.nz

✚ 9G ✉ Intersection of SH1 and SH5, 10km (6 miles) north of Taupo

☎ 03 378 0913 ⚙ Oct–Mar daily 9–5; Apr–Sep 9–4:30 ✋ Moderate

🍴 Café ($); *hangi* as part of evening tour

WAITOMO CAVES

Best places to see, ▶ 54–55.

HOTELS

AUCKLAND

Aachen House Boutique Hotel ($$$)

Five-star luxury bed-and-breakfast hotel in the chic suburb of Remuera, superbly furnished with antiques and porcelain.

✉ 39 Market Road, Remuera ☎ 09 520 2329; www.aachenhouse.co.nz

City Central Hotel ($–$$)

A no-nonsense inexpensive hotel, the City Central is well placed, clean and comfy.

✉ Corner of Wellesley and Albert streets ☎ 09 307 3388; www.citycentralhotel.co.nz

Esplanade Hotel ($$$)

Ten minutes by ferry from the central business district, this luxurious boutique hotel has fine harbour and city views.

✉ 1 Victoria Road, Devonport ☎ 09 445 1291; www.esplanadehotel.co.nz

Great Ponsonby Arthotel ($$$)

The Great Ponsonby is one of the top bed-and-breakfasts in the city, thanks to its personal service and sumptuous breakfasts. The stylish 1890s villa, decorated with works by New Zealand artists, is in a quiet cul-de-sac; it has a green focus, with the option for guests to offset their carbon footprint by planting a kauri tree on Motuine Island in the Hauraki Gulf.

✉ 30 Ponsonby Terrace, Ponsonby ☎ 09 376 5989; www.greatpons.co.nz

BAY OF ISLANDS

Allegra House ($$–$$$)

In the heart of Paihia, with fine views across the bay, this modern home offers bed-and-breakfast or an apartment.

✉ 39 Bayview Road, Paihia ☎ 09 402 7932; www.allegra.co.nz

Copthorne Bay of Islands Hotel ($$–$$$)

Right on the waterfront, in spacious grounds within the Waitangi National Reserve, this hotel has comfortable modern rooms.

✉ Tau Henare Drive, Paihia ☎ 09 402 7411; www.millenniumhotels.co.nz

The Summer House Bed-and-Breakfast ($$$)
Subtropical gardens and a citrus orchard add to the appeal of this popular bed-and-breakfast two minutes from Kerikeri.
✉ 424 Kerikeri Road, Kerikeri ☎ 09 407 4294;
www.thesummerhouse.co.nz

COROMANDEL PENINSULA
Karamana Homestead ($$)
Immerse yourself in the history of the Coromandel by staying in one of the peninsula's oldest homes, dating from 1872. Decorated throughout with antiques, Karamana has just two rooms and a two-bedroom cottage, all wheelchair-accessible.
✉ 84 Whangapoua Road, Coromandel Town ☎ 07 866 7138;
www.karamanahomestead.com

ROTORUA
Millennium Hotel Rotorua ($$–$$$)
This popular chain hotel is located close to the Polynesian Spa, and has a nightly Maori cultural performance and *hangi*.
✉ Corner of Eruera and Hinemaru streets ☎ 07 347 1234;
www.millenniumhotels.co.nz

Regal Palms Motor Lodge ($$–$$$)
One of the best motels in town. Its stylish interior and numerous facilities (including a heated pool, tennis courts, gym and sauna) have helped it earn a five-star Qualmark rating.
✉ 350 Fenton Street ☎ 07 350 3232; www.regalpalms.co.nz

RESTAURANTS
AUCKLAND
Antoine's Restaurant ($$$)
Run by the same chef since 1973, Antoine's has maintained a reputation for top-class New Zealand cuisine cooked in a modern French style. Of the three dinner menus, the 'Nostalgia' menu includes the restaurant's most popular dishes over the years.
✉ 333 Parnell Road ☎ 09 379 8756 🕐 Lunch Wed–Fri, also dinner Mon–Sat. Closed Sun

Cin Cin on Quay ($$$)
See page ➤ 58.

The French Café ($$$)
Multi-award-winning restaurant south of the city centre. If you can't decide, opt for one of the tasting menus.
✉ 210 Symonds Street, Newton ☎ 09 377 1911 🕐 Lunch Mon, dinner Tue–Sat

Iguaçu ($$)
See page ➤ 59.

Mudbrick Restaurant ($$$)
Worth the ferry trip to Waiheke Island alone, and with stunning views of the city, this vineyard restaurant produces consistently top-rate dishes using New Zealand produce.
✉ Church Bay Road, Oneroa, Waiheke Island ✉ 09 372 9050 ✉ Lunch and dinner daily

Oh Calcutta ($$)
This Indian restaurant has been serving dishes from throughout the Indian sub-continent for more than 15 years. In that time it has picked up several awards for its service and authentic cuisine.
✉ 151 Parnell Road, Parnell ☎ 09 377 9090 🕐 Lunch Wed–Fri, dinner daily

Orbit ($$$)
Rotating restaurant at the top of the Sky Tower, with magnificent views and equally impressive cuisine.
✉ Sky Tower, corner of Victoria and Federal streets ☎ 09 363 6000
🕐 Brunch Sat–Sun, lunch Mon–Fri, dinner daily

Pearl Garden Dim Sim Restaurant ($–$$)
One of Auckland's best *dim sum* restaurants, with a popular lunchtime *yum cha* menu. Other choices include standards such as chicken with cashews and beef in oyster sauce.
✉ 1 Teed Street, Newmarket ☎ 09 523 3696 🕐 Daily 11:30–2:30, 5:30–late

Sails Restaurant ($$$)

Popular restaurant set in the southern hemisphere's largest marina, with views of the harbour bridge. Fresh ingredients are the chef's keywords, with a focus on New Zealand seafood.

✉ Westhaven Marina, Westhaven Drive ☎ 09 378 9890 ◷ Lunch Mon–Fri, dinner daily

Sake Bar Rikka ($$)

An authentic Japanese restaurant and sake bar with a range of cooking styles on offer. Choose from tempura, sushi, sashimi, chicken teriyaki and more.

✉ 19 Drake Street, Freemans Bay ☎ 09 377 8239 ◷ Lunch Mon–Fri, dinner Mon–Sat

Soul Bar and Bistro ($$–$$$)

Here you will find top-quality food served in a stylish setting with decks overlooking the beautiful harbour. The seafood, in particular, is excellent.

✉ Viaduct Harbour ☎ 09 356 7249 ◷ Lunch and dinner daily

BAY OF ISLANDS

Kamakura ($$$)

A stylish waterfront restaurant with a reputation for superb food from the Pacific Rim.

✉ 29 The Strand, Russell ☎ 09 403 7771 ◷ Lunch daily Nov–Apr, dinner daily

Marsden Estate ($$)

Eat on the terrace overlooking the vines while enjoying a glass of this winery's top-notch wines. The menu is seasonal and eclectic, with such varied choices as oxtail stew and red Thai chicken curry.

✉ Wiroa Road, Kerikeri ☎ 09 407 9398 ◷ Daily 10–2

Only Seafood ($$–$$$)

Game fish and local Orongo Bay oysters are specialties at this popular restaurant opposite the waterfront.

✉ 40 Marsden Road, Paihia ☎ 09 402 6066 ◷ Dinner daily from 5pm

The Sugar Boat ($$)

Enjoy a drink on the deck of this 1890 lighter (a type of barge used to transfer goods in and out of harbour) before eating down in the hold, now an elegant restaurant.

✉ Waitangi Bridge, Paihia ☎ 09 402 7018 🕐 Daily 5pm–late

COROMANDEL PENINSULA

Peppertree Restaurant and Bar ($$)

Often voted the top restaurant in town, and specializing in seafood. Try the local oysters or green-shell mussels, followed by the fish of the day.

✉ 31 Kapanga Road, Coromandel Town ☎ 07 866 8211 🕐 Daily 11–late

ROTORUA

Bistro 1284 ($$$)

An intimate restaurant, frequently voted Rotorua's best, with a small but varied menu. Asian influences can be seen in dishes like sesame-coated squid with a sweet chilli dressing, or you can select from European-style options like the braised lamb shanks.

✉ 1284 Eruera Street ☎ 07 346 1284 🕐 Dinner daily

Fat Dog ($)

Popular, quirky café with a wide-ranging menu. The breakfasts in particular are worth coming for, ranging from the Fatdog Works to pancakes and lighter options like fresh fruit salad.

✉ 1161 Arawa Street ☎ 07 347 7586 🕐 Sun–Wed 8am–9pm; Thu–Sat 8am–9:30pm

The Pig and Whistle ($–$$)

The pub's name is a tongue-in-cheek reference to the building's former use as a police station. The traditional pub fare of burgers, steaks, and fish and chips can be washed down with Swine Lager.

✉ Corner of Haupapa and Tutanekai streets ☎ 07 347 3025 🕐 Daily 11:30am–late

Sabroso ($$)

The Venezuelan owner of this popular, central restaurant

serves up Latin American dishes and great cocktails.
✉ 1184 Haupapa Street ☎ 07 349 0591 🕔 Dinner daily; closed Wed
in winter

TAUPO
The Brantry ($$$)
Renowned chef Prue Campbell creates modern New Zealand
dishes using local seasonal ingredients.
✉ 45 Rifle Range Road ☎ 07 378 0484 🕔 Dinner daily

The Cottage Café ($$)
All-day breakfasts and brunches are the specialty here, along with
excellent coffee. This is a great place to bring kids – they'll love the
food and the large outdoor area.
✉ 100 Kinloch Road, Kinloch ☎ 07 378 1077 🕔 Dec–Mar Fri–Sat 9:30–9,
Sun–Thu 9:30–4; Apr–Nov Tue–Sun 9:30–4

Edgewater Restaurant ($$$)
Restaurant overlooking the lake at the Millennium Hotel Manuels.
Imaginative New Zealand dishes.
✉ 243 Lake Terrace ☎ 07 378 5110 🕔 Dinner only

SHOPPING

Auckland's main shopping area is along Queen Street, between
Quay Street and Aoatea Square. The major hotels, banks, stores,
art gallery, cinemas, concert halls and information centres are on
or adjacent to this street. There are also many suburban shopping
areas in the city, with Newmarket and the St Lukes Mall in the
suburb of Mount Albert being of special interest. Elsewhere,
Northland and the Coromandel are known for their arts and crafts
outlets, while Rotorua is the centre of Maori arts.

DEPARTMENT AND CLOTHING STORES
Canterbury of New Zealand
New Zealand clothing, smart/casual wear.
✉ Sylvia Park, 286 Mount Wellington Highway, Auckland
☎ 09 573 5521

Kathmandu
Popular New Zealand clothing label, specializing in outdoor wear and camping gear.

✉ 151 Queen Street, Auckland ☎ 09 309 4615

Saks
A fashionable store for getting your hands on exclusive men's and women's international designer clothing.

✉ 254 Broadway, Newmarket, Auckland ☎ 09 520 7630

Smith & Caughey's
Fine department store, including fashion.

✉ 253–261 Queen Street, Auckland ☎ 09 377 4770

Trelise Cooper
Reasonably priced outlet store for one of the country's leading clothes designers.

✉ 536 Parnell Road, Auckland ☎ 09 366 1962

BOOKS AND MAGAZINES

Children's Bookshop
Selected children's books, including titles by a good range of New Zealand authors.

✉ Corner of Jervois and St Marys Bay roads, Ponsonby
☎ 09 376 7283

Dymocks
Main Auckland store for the large Australian bookseller.

✉ 246 Queen Street, Auckland ☎ 09 379 9919

Parsons
Specialist books on the arts and New Zealand.

✉ 26 Wellesley Street East, Auckland ☎ 09 303 1557

Rare Books
One of Auckland's better stores for used non-fiction.

✉ 6 High Street, Auckland ☎ 09 379 0379

MUSIC
Marbecks
Auckland's top shop for serious listening.
✉ 22 Queens Arcade, 34–40 Queen Street, Auckland ☎ 09 379 0444

Real Groovy Records
Selection of new and used records and CDs.
✉ 438 Queen Street, Auckland ☎ 09 302 3940

CRAFTS, ANTIQUES AND MARKETS
Bay of Islands Farmers' Market
Perfect for gathering together the ingredients for a picnic.
✉ Hobson Avenue, Kerikeri ☎ 09 402 6664 🕔 Sun 8:30–noon

Elephant House Crafts
A co-operative selling a variety of handmade New Zealand crafts.
✉ 237 Parnell Road, Parnell, Auckland ☎ 09 309 8740

Otara Market
Early morning, multicultural market with vegetables, domestic items and general merchandise. Some are second-hand.
✉ Newbury Street, Otara ☎ 09 274 0830 🕔 Sat 6am–1pm

Te Puia
Traditional Maori art, created in the New Zealand Maori Arts and Crafts Institute.
✉ Hemo Road, Rotorua ☎ 07 348 9047

Victoria Park Market
A permanent collection of little shops and stallholders selling a range of items, several blocks from the downtown area.
✉ 210 Victoria Street West, Auckland ☎ 09 309 6911

SOUVENIRS
Artport
Portable duty-free New Zealand art at the airport.
✉ Auckland International Airport, Auckland ☎ 09 256 8087

Auckland Museum Shop
The Atrium shop stocks books and toys, while the Foyer shop sells iconic New Zealand gifts.
✉ Auckland Domain, Parnell, Auckland ☎ 09 309 2580

Bay Carving
Carve your own Maori bone pendant as a souvenir of your trip.
✉ The Esplanade, Whitianga, Coromandel ☎ 07 866 4021

Living Nature
Natural skin-care products and cosmetics, 'made from New Zealand'.
✉ SH10, Kerikeri ☎ 09 407 0113

ENTERTAINMENT

CULTURAL ACTIVITIES

Auckland Museum
As well as housing an outstanding collection of objects, the museum offers a daily show of Maori song and dance at 11, 12 and 1:30, plus 2:30 in summer.
✉ Auckland Domain, Parnell, Auckland ☎ 09 306 7048

Auckland Theatre Company
This local theatre group performs at various venues; check the website for details.
✉ 108 Quay Street, Auckland ☎ 09 309 0390; www.atc.co.nz

The Edge
Manages a selection of music and entertainment venues including the Town Hall for concerts, the Aotea Centre, and the Civic Theatre for musicals. Phone for more details.
✉ Aotea Square, Queen Street, Auckland ☎ 09 357 3353

Tamaki Tours
An evening tour combining a *hangi* dinner and a Maori song and dance show in a reconstructed village setting.
✉ 1220 Hinemaru Street, Rotorua ☎ 07 349 2999

Te Puia Maori Arts and Crafts Institute

Maori song and dance performances every day, plus an evening show of storytelling, entertainment and food.

✉ Hemo Road, Rotorua ☎ 07 348 9047 🕒 Oct–Apr daily 8–5; May–Sep 8–4

Waitangi Historic Reserve

Maori cultural performances are held daily at Waitangi in summer and on Saturdays in winter.

✉ Tau Henare Drive, near Paihia ☎ 09 402 7437

NIGHTLIFE

Classic Comedy

Professional comedians and new faces entertain here up to six nights per week.

✉ 321 Queen Street, Auckland ☎ 09 373 4321

Dog's Bollix Bar

Gigs by local bands, jam sessions and regular Irish music nights.

✉ 2 Newton Road, Auckland ☎ 09 376 4600

Family Bar

A gay-friendly venue with regular drag shows, Thu–Sat.

✉ 270 Karangahape Road ☎ 09 309 0213

The Pig and Whistle

This lively bar sells micro-brewed beers. Regular live music.

✉ 1182 Tutanekai Street, Rotorua ☎ 07 347 3025

SKYCITY

Aside from the Sky Tower (▶ 81), two hotels and eight restaurants, the SKYCITY complex is also an entertainment venue. The theatre here hosts international events such as the New Zealand International Comedy Festival, while the casino is open 24 hours a day (over-20s only). The nearby SKYCITY Metro at 297 Queen Street (☎ 09 302 0002) is a 10-screen cinema and IMAX theatre.

✉ Corner of Federal and Victoria streets, Auckland ☎ 09 363 6000

SPORT

Boating

This is a popular Kiwi pastime and there are many boating opportunities across the region. You can go cruising or sailing in the harbours of Auckland, the Hauraki Gulf, the Bay of Islands, the lakes of Rotorua and Lake Taupo.

Fishing

The Rotorua and Taupo areas are famous for trout fishing. Sea-fishing trips, including deep-sea game fishing, are available from most coastal towns, especially in the Bay of Islands.

Golf

Golf courses are found everywhere, and in Rotorua and Taupo, thermal vents can be unusual hazards. The Wairakei International Golf Course (www.wairakeigolfcourse.co.nz), 8km (5 miles) north of Taupo, is recognized as one of the world's best.

Horse racing

Ellerslie Racecourse (www.ellerslie.co.nz) in Auckland is the city's premier racetrack. Race meetings are held about every second or third Saturday and more often at holiday periods.

Walking

There are countless short walking trails, as well as eight long-distance Great Walks through national parks. Details of escorted walks or routes are available from the national park centres. Seek local advice before setting off alone, let someone know where you are going, and always carry warm, all-weather clothing, food, water and maps. For information see: www.doc.govt.nz.

Water sports

Watersports of all kinds can be found throughout New Zealand, either along the extensive coast or on inland lakes and rivers. For those who are less energetic, swimming in the country's hot thermal springs is a relaxing option, as is splashing around on the beaches or lakes.

Lower North Island

South of Lake Taupo the North Island becomes considerably hillier. Tongariro National Park, the oldest national park in New Zealand, is dominated by a trio of volcanoes, marking the southern edge of the volcanic belt.

Wellington

In the west, the city of New Plymouth is watched over by its dormant volcano, Mount Taranaki. In the east, the hills of Hawke's Bay, a horticultural, wine-growing and sheep-farming region, sweep down to the twin cities of Napier and Hastings. In between, the navigable Whanganui River is steeped in Maori history, and you can canoe most of its 290km (180-mile) length and see the country from a different angle. Down at the southern tip of the island lies the vibrant capital city of Wellington, guarding Cook Strait.

Within easy reach of the capital is the Wairarapa, where the small town of Martinborough has several boutique wineries. Beyond, a road leads to Palliser Bay and Cape Palliser, where there are rugged, remote beaches.

WELLINGTON

European settlement started here in 1840 and, since its selection as New Zealand's capital in 1865, Wellington hasn't looked back.

At the southern tip of the North Island, Wellington is a commercial hub with excellent transport links. It's also the nation's cultural centre, home to the New Zealand Symphony Orchestra, the Royal New Zealand Ballet Company, the Museum of New Zealand Te Papa Tongarewa, and a thriving entertainment scene. Bounded on three sides by the sea and inland by circling hills, Wellington is a compact city, easy to get around on foot, and its deep harbour acts as a focal point. There are plenty of parks, gardens and hilly viewpoints, in addition to the beaches.

Within Wellington there is the distinctive heart, including its parliament and government offices; the Hutt Valley – largely residential, but with industry at its southern end; and the northern satellite city of Porirua and the beaches of the Kapiti Coast.

www.wellingtonnz.com

➕ 8L

ℹ️ Civic Square, corner of Victoria and Wakefield streets ☎ 04 802 4860

Botanic Garden

Spread over 25ha (62 acres), this garden includes both native bush and exotic plants. Highlights are the Lady Norwood Rose Garden and Begonia House. At the top of the hill (near the Cable Car terminal) is the **Carter Observatory,** with a planetarium.

www.wellington.govt.nz

✚ *Wellington 1c* ✉ Tinakori Road, Glenmore Street and Upland Road ☎ 04 499 1400 🕙 Daily dawn–dusk 👋 Free 🚌 Cable Car, No 3 Karori bus

Carter Observatory

✉ 40 Salamanca Road ☎ 04 472 8167; **www.**carterobservatory.org 🕙 Daily 10–5 👋 Moderate 🚌 Cable Car

Cable Car

A cable car rises from the terminal off Lambton Quay and at the top are fine views and the appealing **Cable Car Museum.**

www.wellingtoncablecar.co.nz

✚ *Wellington 1d–3d* ✉ Cable Car Lane, 280 Lambton Quay ☎ 04 472 2199 🕙 Mon–Fri 7am–10pm, Sat 8:30am–10pm, Sun and public holidays 9am–10pm, every 10 minutes 👋 Inexpensive

Cable Car Museum

✉ Upper Cable Car terminus, Upland Road, Kelburn ☎ 04 475 3578; www.cablecarmuseum.co.nz 🕙 Nov–Apr daily 9:30–5:30; rest of year 9:30–5 👋 Free

Katherine Mansfield Birthplace

New Zealand's greatest short-story writer was born in this wooden house in 1888. Now restored, the building is open for viewing and has both permament and changing exhibitions.

www.katherinemansfield.com

✚ *Wellington 3a (off map)* ✉ 25 Tinakori Road, Thorndon ☎ 04 473 7268 🕙 Tue–Sun 10–4 👋 Inexpensive 🚌 No 14 Wilton bus

Museum of New Zealand Te Papa Tongarewa
Best places to see, ➤ 40–41.

Museum of Wellington City and Sea
Displays on the history of Wellington city and harbour.
More than 80 model ships, nautical paraphernalia, old
photos and lots more, all illustrating the long maritime
associations of the region.

www.museumofwellington.co.nz

✚ *Wellington 3d* ✉ Queens Wharf ☎ 04 472 8904 🕐 Daily 10–5
✋ Free

National Library and Archives New Zealand
The National Library contains reference copies of books and
periodicals. An important part of the archive is the famous
Alexander Turnbull Library, which includes perhaps the world's
finest collection of works by John Milton, the English poet.

   Nearby is Archives New Zealand, storing important historical
documents, paintings, photographs and films. Exhibitions include
a permanent display of the original 1840 Treaty of Waitangi.

Library
✚ *Wellington 3b* ✉ Corner of Molesworth and Aitken streets
☎ 04 474 3000; www.natlib.govt.nz 🕐 Mon–Fri 9–5, Sat 9–1
🍴 Café Littera ($) ✋ Free

Archives New Zealand
✚ *Wellington 4b* ✉ 10 Mulgrave Street ☎ 04 499 5595;
www.archives.govt.nz 🕐 Mon–Fri 9–5, Sat 9–1 ✋ Free

Old St Paul's Church
The old church, consecrated in 1866, so called to distinguish it
from the new 1964 cathedral, is used mainly for weddings and
concerts. However, its fine Gothic Revival style and its history
have secured it as a property of the Historic Places Trust,
safeguarding its future.

✚ *Wellington 4b* ✉ 34 Mulgrave Street ☎ 04 473 6722;
www.historic.org.nz ⏱ Daily 10–5. Closed Good Fri, 25 Dec
✋ Free; donations welcome

Parliament Buildings

The most distinctive of the Parliament Buildings complex in downtown Wellington is the Beehive, designed by Sir Basil Spence. It houses ministerial offices and the Cabinet Room. Next to it is the Parliament House, home of New Zealand's one-chamber parliament, and adjacent to this is the Parliamentary Library.

www.parliament.nz

✚ *Wellington 3b* ✉ Pathway leads in from Lambton Quay
☎ 04 817 9503 ⏱ Mon–Fri 9–5, Sat and public holidays 9:30–4, Sun 11:30–4. Free daily one-hour tours on the hour ✋ Free ❓ Not open for unguided sightseers

Around Wellington

DAYS BAY AND EASTBOURNE

Although these village suburbs, nestling on hilly slopes on the eastern shores of Wellington's harbour, are connected to the city by road and ferry, they feel a world away. The two beaches are 15 minutes' walk apart. Behind Eastbourne village, with its cafés and craft and antiques shops, the Butterfly Creek trail is a popular local walk, while Williams Park, behind Days Bay, is great for picnics and has a tea room, a pond and tennis courts.

➕ 8L 🍴 Cobar Restaurant, Days Bay ($$$) 🚌 81, 83 via Petone ⛴ The Dominion Post Ferry from Queens Wharf (Up to 16 sailings per day)

FELL LOCOMOTIVE MUSEUM, FEATHERSTON

The fell engine at Featherston is a steam locomotive that was used on the railway over the Rimutaka Range, before the tunnel was built in 1955. The **Rimutaka Rail Trail** follows the route of the former line from the edge of the Wellington conurbation. At 18km (11 miles), the walk takes four to five hours to complete.

www.fellmuseum.org.nz

➕ 9L (Featherston) ✉ Corner of Lyon and Fitzherbert streets, Featherston
☎ 06 308 9379 🕐 Daily 10–4 💵 Inexpensive

Rimutaka Rail Trail

☎ 04 384 7770 (Department of Conservation, Wellington office)

KAPITI COAST

Centred on the suburbs of Paekakariki and Paraparaumu to the north of Wellington, the Kapiti Coast is known for its fine white sandy beaches and good water-sports facilities. Kapiti Island, 5km (3 miles) offshore, is a bird sanctuary with restricted access. Boat trips depart from Paraparaumu. **Southward Car Museum,** near Paraparaumu, has one of the largest and most extensive private collections of vintage automobiles in the southern hemisphere. It's also home to a selection of engines and motorcycles.

✚ 8L 🚆 Plimmerton, Paekakariki or Paraparaumu then buses 71–74
ℹ️ Coastlands Car Park ☎ 04 298 8195; www.naturecoast.co.nz
Southward Car Museum
✉️ Otaihanga Road, Paraparaumu; 55km (33 miles) north of Wellington
☎ 04 297 1221; www.thecarmuseum.co.nz 🕐 Daily 9–4:30. Closed Good Fri,
25 Dec 🍴 Tea room ($) 🖐️ Inexpensive

MOUNT VICTORIA LOOKOUT

Rising from Wellington's inner suburbs, this 196m (643ft) peak
offers a splendid view of the city and harbour. Its Maori name,
Tangi-te-keo, comes from the spirit of a dead *taniwha* (monster)
that was transformed into a *keo* (bird) and flew here to mourn.
Walk or drive to the top.
✚ *Wellington 4f (off map)* 🖐️ Free 🚌 20

OTARI–WILTON'S BUSH

New Zealand's largest collection of indigenous plants is cultivated here in parkland and gardens. Habitats include native bush, natural forest, an alpine garden and a fernery.

www.wellington.govt.nz

➕ *Wellington 1a (off map)* ✉ Wilton Road, Wilton ☎ 04 499 1400 🕒 Daily
✋ Free 🚌 No 14 Wilton bus

PUKAHA MOUNT BRUCE

New Zealand's National Wildlife Centre is a sanctuary for endangered species such as kiwi, tuatara and takahe.

www.mtbruce.org.nz

➕ 9K ✉ 30km (19 miles) north of Masterton ☎ 06 375 8004 🕒 Daily 9–4:30 🍴 Café Takahe ($) ✋ Moderate

THENEWDOWSE, LOWER HUTT

This exciting gallery is a showcase of New Zealand design, with works ranging from contemporary crafts to paintings and traditional Maori carvings. There is a changing programme of events, including talks and musical performances.

www.dowse.org.nz

➕ 8L (Lower Hutt) ✉ 45 Laings Road ☎ 04 570 6500 🕒 Mon–Fri 10–4:30, Sat–Sun 10–5 ✋ Free 🍴 Café Reka ($$) 🚌 81, 83, 91
🚉 Melling Station

ZEALANDIA: THE KARORI SANCTUARY EXPERIENCE

This 225ha (556-acre) mainland 'island', just beyond Wellington's Botanic Garden (▶ 111), has been predator-proofed to provide a haven for native animals such as kiwi, tuatara and weta. The Sanctuary by Night tour is particularly memorable.

www.visitzealandia.com

✚ *Wellington 1e (off map)* ✉ Waiapu Road, Kelburn ☎ 04 920 9200
🕑 Daily 10–5 💷 Moderate 🚌 3, 18

a drive around Wellington

Wellington's Marine Drive starts on Oriental Parade, near the eastern end of Courtenay Place. Note the many narrow and one-way streets in the city centre.

Once on Oriental Parade, continue around Oriental Bay past Mount Victoria (▶ 115).

To drive up Mount Victoria, take Majoribanks Street opposite Courtenay Place then follow signs along the narrow streets to the Admiral Byrd Memorial and Lookout.

Follow Oriental Parade around Point Jerningham into Evans Bay, passing boating facilities and slipways. Turn left onto Cobham Drive, passing the northern end of the airport runway, then keep left out to the next point.

Shelly Bay Road follows the other side of Evans Bay to Point Halswell. Note the Massey Memorial to former Prime Minister William Ferguson Massey (1856–1925).

The route continues past Scorching, Karaka and Worser bays. Continue through Seatoun and the Pass of Branda to rejoin the coast.

Breaker Bay Road follows a bleak stretch of coastline at the harbour entrance. Offshore is Barrett Reef, the craggy rocks where the *Wanganella* ran aground in 1947 and the inter-island ferry *Wahine* foundered in 1968. Moa Point Road leads to the southern end of the airport runway. Continue around Lyall Bay to Island Bay for more views out across Cook Strait.

Return to the city either via Happy Valley and Ohiro or Brooklyn roads to Willis Street and Lambton Quay, or via The Parade and Adelaide Road back to Cambridge Terrace and Courtenay Place.

Distance 40km (25 miles)
Time 2.5 hours
Start/end point Courtenay Place ✚ *Wellington 4f*
Lunch Elements ($$) ✉ 144 Onepu Road, Lyall Bay ☎ 04 939 1292
🕐 Lunch daily, dinner Tue–Sat

More to see in the Lower North Island

NAPIER

Hawke's Bay is a picturesque region of hills sweeping down to the central east coast, a fertile plain popularly known as 'the fruit bowl of New Zealand'. It is also a thriving wine producer, with a number of older vineyards. Tragically, the twin cities of Napier and Hastings suffered a devastating earthquake in 1931.

The rebuilding of Napier in the contemporary architecture of the time has made its fascinating art deco design a real attraction, celebrated each February in a festival, and the traffic-free streets in the town create a pleasant shopping environment.

✚ 10J
ℹ 100 Marine Parade ☎ 06 834 1911

Cape Kidnappers

The world's largest known mainland colony of Australasian gannets lies 32km (20 miles) southwest of Napier at the southernmost tip of Hawke Bay, so named by Captain Cook when local Maori attempted to kidnap a Tahitian boy on the *Endeavour*. These large seabirds arrive in July and lay their eggs in October and November; these hatch about six weeks later. The best time to visit the reserve is between November and February.

✚ 10J ✉ Access by tour or on foot (tides permitting) 🖐 Tours expensive; reserve locally

Marine Parade

Attractions along Napier's esplanade include **Hawke's Bay Museum and Art Gallery,** which has an interesting audiovisual section on the 1931 earthquake. Other intriguing displays include one devoted to local Maori culture and another to art deco in the region.

At the **National Aquarium of New Zealand** is a huge oceanarium housing 1,500 fish, including several species of sharks. Divers brave enough can even join the inmates. Other tanks house freshwater species, seahorses and corals, and there is also a kiwi house, where the shy nocturnal birds are kept in natural surroundings along with tuatara, lizards and an Australian saltwater crocodile.

Hawke's Bay Museum and Art Gallery
☎ 06 835 7781; www.hbmag.co.nz
🕐 Fri–Wed 10–6, Thu 10–8
✋ Inexpensive

National Aquarium of New Zealand
☎ 06 834 1404;
www.nationalaquarium.co.nz
🕐 Daily 9–5 ✋ Moderate

Te Mata Peak

A narrow road climbs via Havelock North to the top of this 399m (1,309ft) viewpoint, offering a spectacular panorama over the Heretaunga Plains. The peak forms part of the 98ha (242 acre) Te Mata Peak Trust Park, and has good walking routes.

➕ 10J ✉ Te Mata Peak Road; 31km (19 miles) south of Napier
ℹ Havelock North Village Information
☎ 06 877 9600

NEW PLYMOUTH

With the development of oil and gas reserves in the region, the city of New Plymouth, in northern Taranaki, has come to be known as the 'energy capital'. The fertile volcanic soils around Mount Taranaki, the region's dominant landmark, support a thriving dairy industry, along with the gardens for which the district has become renowned.

The annual Taranaki Rhododendron and Garden Festival (Oct–Nov) attracts visitors from around the country and abroad, as does WOMAD: World of Music, Arts and Dance (Mar).

www.newplymouthnz.com

✚ 7H

ℹ Puke Ariki Museum and Library, Ariki Street ☎ 06 759 6080

Govett-Brewster Art Gallery

New Zealand's main contemporary art museum focuses on works by up-and-coming national and Pacific Rim artists. Its collections include work by modernist artist Len Lye (1901–80), whose *Wind Wand* sculpture is on New Plymouth's waterfront.

www.govettbrewster.com

✉ 42 Queen Street ☎ 06 759 6060 ⏰ Daily 10–5 🍴 Café ($) ✋ Free

Mount Taranaki

Visible from New Plymouth and most parts of the Taranaki region, Mount Taranaki, previously known as Mount Egmont, rises 2,518m (8,259ft) in an impressive near-perfect cone from the coastal plain. Captain Cook sighted the volcano in 1770, naming it for the Earl of Egmont, former first Lord of the Admiralty.

The surrounding Egmont National Park has a small winter ski-field and several walking trails. The weather conditions can be unpredictable, but this does not deter the climbers who visit.

✚ 7H ✋ Free

ℹ Egmont National Park Visitor Centre, Egmont Road ☎ 06 756 0990

⏰ Daily 8–4:30

Pukekura Park

Chief among many parks in New Plymouth, these gardens have fountains, a fernery, woodland and two lakes.

Adjoining Pukekura Park, but separated by a concert bowl, is the more formal Brooklands Park, where there is a rhododendron dell and European-style flower gardens, as well as a small zoo (free).

✉ Fillis Street, New Plymouth 🕐 Nov–Apr daily 7:30–8; Mar–Oct 7:30–7

✋ Free

ℹ Puke Ariki Museum and Library, Ariki Street ☎ 06 759 6060

TONGARIRO NATIONAL PARK

Best places to see, ► 38–39.

HOTELS

WELLINGTON

Ascot Cottage ($$–$$$)

Built in the late 1800s, this self-contained one-bedroom cottage is in the heart of historic Thorndon. The facilities are comprehensive, and a Continental breakfast is included in the rate.

✉ Ascot Street, Thorndon ☎ 04 479 3721; www.ascotcottage.co.nz

Copthorne Hotel Wellington Oriental Bay ($$–$$$)

Visitors who revel in having a five-star view will love this hillside hotel. And it's just a two-minute walk to Te Papa and lively Courtenay Place.

✉ 100 Oriental Parade ☎ 04 385 0279; www.kingsgateorientalbay.co.nz

Hotel InterContinental ($$$)

This striking, bronze-coloured building is a city landmark, near the Lambton Quay shops, Parliament and a major sports stadium. It has the same high standards as other members of the chain, and facilities include two restaurants (➤ 126) and a health club.

✉ 2 Grey Street ☎ 04 472 2722; www.wellington.intercontinental.com

The Wellesley Hotel ($$$)

The 1920s neo-Georgian Wellesley is a splendidly restored heritage building which has plenty of character and is set in the heart of the Lambton quarter.

✉ 2–8 Maginnity Street ☎ 04 474 1308; www.thewellesley.co.nz

YHA Wellington City ($)

With rooms ranging from shared dormitories with four beds to deluxe private ensuite doubles, this hostel near Courteney Place is a great choice for travellers on a budget.

✉ 292 Wakefield Street ☎ 04 801 7280; www.yha.co.nz

NAPIER

County Hotel ($$$)

This Edwardian hotel, located in the middle of town, was one of the few buildings that survived the 1931 earthquake. It has 18 suites and rooms, and a restaurant (► 128) and bar.

✉ 12 Browning Street ☎ 06 835 7800; www.countyhotel.co.nz

McHardy Lodge ($$$)

High on a hill above Napier, the 1891 McHardy Lodge has been turned into a luxury boutique hotel with six suites.

✉ 11 Bracken Street ☎ 06 835 0605; www.mchardylodge.com

NEW PLYMOUTH

Airlie House Bed & Breakfast ($$)

This 120-year-old villa, five minutes' walk from the waterfront and attractions, has two bedrooms with private bathrooms, and a self-contained studio apartment.

✉ 161 Powderham Street ☎ 06 757 8866; www.airliehouse.co.nz

The Nice Hotel ($$$)

Art and history are the themes of this offbeat boutique hotel in the 1860s former Redcoats Hospital building. The restaurant here is also recommended (► 129).

✉ 71 Brougham Street ☎ 06 758 6423; www.nicehotel.co.nz

TONGARIRO NATIONAL PARK

Chateau Tongariro ($$–$$$)

The grand neo-Georgian Chateau Tongariro, on the slopes of Mount Ruapehu, was built in 1929. Go walking in summer and skiing in winter, or play billiards, tennis or boules.

✉ Whakapapa ☎ 07 892 3809; www.chateau.co.nz

RESTAURANTS

WELLINGTON

Arbitrageur ($$$)

The Mediterranean dishes on the menu in this elegant restaurant are colour-coded to make wine selection from the list of 600-plus national and international labels easier.

✉ 125 Featherston Street ☎ 04 499 5530; www.arbitrageur.co.nz ✪ Lunch and dinner Mon–Fri, dinner only Sat

Backbencher ($$)

Right across the street from the Parliament Buildings (➤ 113), this pub is popular with MPs, whom it satirizes in its menu. Opt for J Key's chicken breast or, if your allegiances rest with his predecessor, H Clark's skin-on *tarakihi* (pan-fried fish).

✉ 34 Molesworth Street ☎ 04 472 3065 🕓 Lunch and dinner daily

Caffe l'Affare ($)

This thriving coffee business and café was established in 1990, and remains popular with locals and visitors alike. Aside from its excellent coffee, the café serves light dishes such as all-day breakfasts and open sandwiches.

✉ 27 College Street ☎ 04 385 9748 🕓 Mon–Fri 7am–4:30, Sat 8am–4

Chameleon ($$$)

Combine top hotel dining with a delicious menu at the InterContinental. Dinner choices include Akaroa salmon, ostrich fillet, and pumpkin and hazelnut strudel.

✉ 2 Grey Street ☎ 04 495 7841 🕓 Daily 6:30am–late

The Flying Burrito Brothers ($$)

Popular Mexican cantina and tequileria. Fabulous fajitas, tasty tacos and marvellous margueritas. There's a children's menu too.

✉ Corner of Cuba and Vivian streets ☎ 04 385 8811 🕓 Dinner daily

Hippotamus ($$$)

Top-class cuisine in a boutique hotel opposite Te Papa. Spoil yourself by dropping in for a divine high tea (bookings essential).

✉ Museum Hotel, 90 Cable Street ☎ 04 802 8935 🕓 Breakfast, lunch, high tea and dinner daily

Lido Café ($$)

For breakfast and lunch, sit at a pavement table of this busy café. The 1959 Racing Conference Building that houses the café is a Wellington landmark, with yellow tiles and horseshoe motifs.

✉ 81–85 Victoria Street ☎ 04 499 6666 🕓 Tue–Fri 7:30–late, Mon 7:30–3, Sat–Sun 9–late

Logan Brown ($$$)

Steve Logan and Al Brown are laid-back hosts with a passion for food, and for New Zealand ingredients in particular. Dishes such as rack of Hawke's Bay lamb, Canterbury venison and hot smoked snapper helped win the pair *Cuisine* magazine's supreme Restaurant of the Year award in 2009.

✉ 192 Cuba Street ☎ 04 801 5114 ⏰ Lunch and dinner Mon–Fri, dinner only Sat–Sun

Matterhorn ($$–$$$)

See page ➤ 59.

Shed 5 ($$$)

Elegant dining in a converted woolstore with great views over the waterfront. Seafood is a specialty, including crispy tempura fish and catch of the day with truffle soy sauce.

✉ Queens Wharf ☎ 04 499 9069 ⏰ Mon–Fri 11:30–10:30, Sat–Sun 10am–10:30pm

Thai Chef's Restaurant ($$)

Popular with Wellingtonians (including staff at the Royal Thai Embassy) for its authentic Thai cuisine.

✉ 1 Blair Street ☎ 04 385 4535 ⏰ Lunch Wed–Fri, dinner daily

White House ($$$)

Fine dining with harbour views; the restaurant mainly features New Zealand cuisine.

✉ 232 Oriental Parade ☎ 04 385 8555 ⏰ Summer: lunch Mon–Fri, dinner daily. Winter: lunch Fri, dinner Mon–Sat

GREYTOWN
Bar Saluté ($$)

Choose from a selection of tapas dishes, or one of their home-made pizzas. Not surprisingly for this wine-growing area, the bar has a good list of local labels, as well as international wines, beers, sangria and sherry.

✉ 83 Main Street ☎ 06 304 9825 ⏰ Wed–Sun 12–late

Café Trends ($–$$)

Light lunch selections, including paninis, through to more substantial dishes such as braised lamb shanks and pan-fried blue cod.

✉ Main Street North ☎ 06 304 8550 ⏰ Daily 8:30–3

NAPIER

Chambers ($$$)

New Zealand cuisine, such as rack of lamb and roast venison, in the historic County Hotel, dating from 1909. The building was one of the few to survive the 1931 Hawke's Bay earthquake (➤ 120).

✉ County Hotel, 12 Browning Street ☎ 06 835 7800 ⏰ Dinner daily

Church Road Winery ($$)

Beautifully cooked seasonal dishes can be accompanied by a glass or two of this vineyard's award-winning wines.

✉ 150 Church Road, Taradale ☎ 06 844 2053 ⏰ Oct–Apr daily 11:30–3:30; May–Sep Tue–Sun 11:30–3:30

Clive Square Café ($)

The best breakfasts in town, made with the freshest Hawke's Bay ingredients.

✉ 7 Clive Square ☎ 06 835 3091 ⏰ Mon–Sat 8:30–3:30

Mission Estate ($$$)

Fresh, seasonal cooking within the setting of New Zealand's oldest winery. You can dine inside in the former seminary building or outside on the terrace, soaking up views to Napier and beyond.

✉ 198 Church Road, Taradale ☎ 06 845 9354; www.missionestate.co.nz ⏰ Daily 10am–late

New Bangkok House ($$)

Reasonably priced Thai cuisine. The dishes are authentic and beautifully cooked, and can be washed down with a glass of Thai beer.

✉ 205 Dickens Street, Napier ☎ 06 835 5335 ⏰ Lunch and dinner Tue–Sun

Pacifica ($$$)

This small restaurant (it seats only 35) creates innovative French-influenced dishes, many based around fresh local seafood. The daily menu includes such options as whole baked flounder and quail stuffed with lamb sweetbreads.

✉ 209 Marine Parade ☎ 06 833 6335 ⊕ Dinner Mon–Fri

NEW PLYMOUTH
Salt ($$)

Stunning sea views and Pacific Rim food in New Plymouth's Waterfront Hotel. Come for a buffet breakfast, a light salad or sandwich for lunch, or more substantial meat or fish dishes in the evening.

✉ Waterfront Hotel, 1 Egmont Street ☎ 06 769 5301; www.waterfront.co.nz
⊕ Daily 7am–10pm

Table Restaurant ($$$)

One of the best restaurants in New Plymouth, for both its food and service. Dine inside or on the outdoor deck, choosing from such dishes as duck spring rolls and braised South Island rabbit.

✉ Nice Hotel, 71 Brougham Street ☎ 06 758 6423 ⊕ Dinner daily

TONGARIRO NATIONAL PARK
Ruapehu Restaurant ($$$)

Classic dishes with a Pacific Rim twist, in the sophisticated surroundings of one of New Zealand's best-known hotels.

✉ Chateau Tongariro, Whakapapa ☎ 07 892 3809 ⊕ Dinner daily

SHOPPING

The capital's main shopping street is Lambton Quay, but Willis Street, Manners Street and Cuba Street are also of interest, with local designer stores. There is an underground shopping mall at the corner of Lambton Quay and Willis Street. Post offices, banks, libraries, theatres and visitor information are close by.

Napier offers a smart downtown shopping area and New Plymouth shopping is centred on its main street (Devon Street). One block north, the City Centre Mall offers enclosed shopping.

DEPARTMENT AND CLOTHING STORES
Kirkcaldie & Stains
Elegant department store, established in 1863.

✉ 165–177 Lambton Quay, Wellington ☎ 04 472 5899

Starfish
Designer clothes and accessories, 100 per cent New Zealand made.

✉ 128 Willis Street, Wellington ☎ 04 385 3722; www.starfish.co.nz

BOOKS AND MAGAZINES
Quilter's Bookshop
Treasure trove of rare and historic volumes.

✉ 110 Lambton Quay, Wellington ☎ 04 472 2767

Unity Books
Specialist retailer committed to New Zealand publishing.

✉ 57 Willis Street, Wellington ☎ 04 499 4245

MUSIC
Parsons Books & Music
A serious bookshop with classical CDs as well.

✉ 126 Lambton Quay, Wellington ☎ 04 472 4587

Slow Boat Records
Specialist in rare titles, from the 1950s to today.

✉ 183 Cuba Street, Wellington ☎ 04 385 1330

CRAFTS, ANTIQUES AND MARKETS
Hawke's Bay Farmers' Market
One of the best farmers' markets in the country, with food to eat here, pack for a picnic or take home as a souvenir.

✉ A&P Showgrounds, Kenilworth Street, Hastings
☎ www.foodhawkesbay.co.nz ⦿ Sun 8:30–12:30

McGregor Wright Gallery
Art dealer that specializes predominantly in New Zealand artists.

✉ Corner of Raumati Road and SH1, Raumati, Kapiti Coast ☎ 04 299 4958

Soup
Pre-loved designer clothes hang alongside beautiful vintage garments, all on sale at knock-down prices.

✉ 8 Blair Street, Wellington ☎ 04 385 4722

Walker & Hall Fine Gifts
A jewellery shop and silversmith that has been established for more than a century.

✉ 148 Lambton Quay, Wellington ☎ 04 473 9266

SOUVENIRS
Iko Iko
Quirky Kiwiana gifts, ranging from toys to tikis to tea towels.

✉ 118 Cuba Mall, Wellington ☎ 04 385 9077

Jewellery Arts Studio
Fine-quality studio-made jewellery in traditional Maori designs ready to take home with you.

✉ Cable Car Lane, 286 Lambton Quay, Wellington ☎ 04 472 8866

Sommerfields
Native wood, ceramics, wool and possum products – all made in New Zealand.

✉ 296 Lambton Quay, Wellington ☎ 04 499 4847

ENTERTAINMENT

CULTURAL ACTIVITIES
Downstage Theatre
Highly regarded as Wellington's best playhouse. Details of events can be obtained by calling ahead of your visit.

✉ 12 Cambridge Terrace, Wellington ☎ 04 801 6946

Michael Fowler Centre
The leading concert venue in Wellington is the Michael Fowler Centre, which is also home to the New Zealand Symphony Orchestra.

✉ 111 Wakefield Street, Wellington ☎ 04 801 4231

TheNewDowse

One of the best art galleries in the Wellington region. It also hosts talks, workshops and other events.

✉ 45 Laings Road, Lower Hutt ☎ 04 570 6500 🕐 Mon–Fri 10–4:30, Sat–Sun 10–5

St James Theatre

Home of the Royal New Zealand Ballet, and the venue for events ranging from rock concerts to children's plays.

✉ 77–87 Courteney Place, Wellington ☎ 04 802 4060

NIGHTLIFE

Bar Bodega

Bar Bodega is dedicated to real ale and good music.

✉ 101 Ghuznee Street, Wellington ☎ 04 384 8212

The Establishment

Whether you want to dance until late, listen to jazz or watch the big match, you can do it here.

✉ Corner of Courtenay Place and Blair Street, Wellington
☎ 04 382 8654

Good Luck

Dance club and bar fashioned like a Chinese opium den. Live music plus resident DJ.

✉ Basement, 126 Cuba Street, Wellington ☎ 04 801 9950

Happy

A relaxed basement venue with nightly gigs of jazz and alternative live music.

✉ 118 Tory Street, Wellington ☎ 04 384 1965

SPORT

Skiing

The North Island's major ski-fields (July to September, although sometimes longer) are on the northern and southwestern slopes of Mount Ruapehu in Tongariro National Park.

Upper South Island

Despite being one-third larger in area than the North Island, the South Island has only one-quarter of the country's population. The scenery is internationally renowned for its beauty and variety.

Christchurch

At the top of South Island are three outstanding national parks for visitors to the country to explore: the Abel Tasman National Park, with its beautiful coastline and beaches; and the Kahurangi and Nelson Lakes national parks, characterized by remote bush, mountain scenery and abundant birdlife. To the east are the world-renowned vineyards of Marlborough and the stunning bays of the Marlborough Sounds, while the sea offshore here teems with whales, dolphins and seals.

Christchurch is the South Island's international gateway and also claims the title of its largest city. Considered the most 'English' of New Zealand's cities, it stands on the edge of the Canterbury Plains.

CHRISTCHURCH

Christchurch was founded as a Church of England colony in 1850, and much of its attraction rests with those colonial beginnings, the graceful lines of some of its early neo-Gothic stone buildings contrasting with those of more contemporary design. The city is named after England's Christ Church College, Oxford, where the city's founding father was educated.

Much of interest lies in the compact downtown area, bisected by the willow-lined Avon River, complete with ducks, ornate bridges, boatsheds and punts, and centred on the cathedral and its lively square. Beyond the city centre, numerous parks and gardens grace the flat suburbs, giving Christchurch the nickname of Garden City. To the southeast, the Port Hills separate the city from its port at Lyttelton, while beyond, on Banks Peninsula, is New Zealand's only French settlement, Akaroa.

The city makes a good base for exploring. Many long-distance bus tours start and finish here, and day trips include swimming at Hanmer's hot springs (➤ 141), whale-watching at Kaikoura (➤ 146–147), taking a train through the Southern Alps (➤ 50–51), skiing in winter, or visiting Aoraki/Mount Cook, New Zealand's highest mountain.

www.christchurch.nz.com

➕ 5S

ℹ️ Old Chief Post Office Building, Cathedral Square

☎ 03 379 9629

Arts Centre

Hosting a weekend craft and food market, with live entertainment, this complex, once part of the university, is equally worth visiting on weekdays. Stores, workshops and galleries sell and display arts and craft works, making it a good place to look for gifts.

www.artscentre.org.nz

✉ 2 Worcester Boulevard ☎ 03 366 0989 🕐 Daily 10–5
✋ Free 🍽 Four cafés ($) and two restaurants ($$–$$$)
🚋 Christchurch Tram

Avon River

This stream adds a restful charm to the city as it meanders through Christchurch, and there are walks along its banks. Boats, punts and canoes can be rented – enquire at the **Antigua Boat Sheds.**

The Town Hall complex (➤ 156) here includes a concert hall, theatre, conference rooms and restaurant.

Antigua Boat Sheds

✉ 2 Cambridge Terrace ☎ 03 366 0337; www.punting.co.nz
🕐 Oct–Apr daily 9–6; May–Sep 10–4 ✋ Moderate
🍽 Boatshed Café ($) 🚋 Christchurch Tram

Botanic Gardens

The 30ha (74 acre) Botanic Gardens lie within Hagley Park, a vast sports and recreation area on the fringe of the central business district. Set amid the wooded lawns are a number of themed gardens, and there are many displays of flowering trees and exotic plants.

✉ Rolleston Avenue ☎ 03 941 8999; www.ccc.govt.nz/parks (tours) 🕐 Gardens: daily 7am to 1 hour before sunset; conservatories: 10:15–4; guided tours mid-Sep to Apr daily 1:30
🍽 Botanic Gardens Café ($); Curator's House Restaurant ($$$)
🚋 Christchurch Tram

Canterbury Museum

This is a general collection relating to New Zealand history and ethnology. Two specialist exhibits are: The Moa Hunters, with life-size dioramas of early Maori and the giant flightless bird (long extinct); and the excellent Hall of Antarctic Discovery, with relics from the Scott expedition and others. There are free guided tours Tuesdays and Thursdays.

www.canterburymuseum.com

✉ Rolleston Avenue ☎ 03 366 5000 🕓 Oct–Mar daily 9–5:30; Apr–Sep 9–5 ✋ Free; charges for some exhibits 🍴 Museum Café ($) 🚌 Christchurch Tram ❓ One-hour free guided tours Tue, Thu 3:30

Canterbury Provincial Council Buildings

Built in 1858 beside the Avon River, this Gothic Revival complex reflects the city's English heritage and the early days when New Zealand had 13 independent provinces.

✉ Corner of Durham and Armagh streets ☎ 03 941 7680 🕓 Tours Mon–Sat 10:30–3:30 ✋ Free 🚌 Christchurch Tram

Christchurch Art Gallery

Opened in this new venue in 2003, the gallery exhibits modern New Zealand and British paintings, as well as a range of other works of art, including ceramics, Maori craft and photography.

✉ Corner of Montreal Street and Worcester Boulevard ☎ 03 941 7300 🕓 Thu–Tue 10–5, Wed 10–9 ✋ Free; charges for some exhibitions 🍴 Alchemy Café & Wine Bar ($$) 🚌 Christchurch Tram

Christchurch Cathedral

The building of this Gothic Revival edifice, crowned with a 63m (207ft) copper-clad spire, began in 1864 and finished 40 years later.

There are 134 steep steps to the top of the bell tower but the views from the top are worth it.

www.christchurchcathedral.co.nz

✉ Cathedral Square ☎ 03 366 0046 🕐 Oct–Mar daily 8:30–7; Apr–Sep 9–5. Tower closed until 11:30am Sun ✋ Free; tower inexpensive 🍴 Café ($)

🚌 Christchurch Tram ❓ Free guided tours Mon–Fri 11, 2, Sat 11, Sun 11:30

Christchurch Tram

Electric trams first came to Christchurch in 1905 but the network closed in the early 1950s. Now, restored vintage trams take tourists on a scenic route through the city, taking in many of the best sights. Tickets are valid for two days, and passengers can hop on and off to suit.

www.tram.co.nz

✉ From Cathedral Square

☎ 03 366 7830 🕐 Nov–Mar daily 9–9; Apr–Oct 9–6

✋ Moderate

Science Alive!

In the old Christchurch railway station, this modern interactive science facility offers an educational yet fun-filled experience for people of all ages.

www.sciencealive.co.nz

✉ 392 Moorhouse Avenue

☎ 03 365 5199 🕐 Daily 10–5

✋ Moderate 🚌 Red Bus free shuttle

a walk in Christchurch

Start at the visitor information centre in Cathedral Square, pausing to take a look at the cathedral (► 136).

Stroll due west along Worcester Street to the Avon River (► 135). The Bridge of Remembrance to the left was built to commemorate Kiwi troops who died during World War I.

Pass the Christchurch Art Gallery (► 136) and cross Montreal Street, then pause at the Arts Centre (► 135). On weekends, when there are outdoor stalls to browse as well as the many shops, allow extra time. Next, the Canterbury Museum (► 136) looms in front.

Continue for two blocks north on Rolleston Avenue, passing Christ's College, and turn east onto Armagh Street. Pass Cranmer Square.

At the Durham Street intersection, note the architecture of the Canterbury Provincial Council Buildings (► 136).

Cross the Avon again to enter Victoria Square. Across the square, past statues and a fountain, note the award-winning (1972) architecture of the Town Hall.

Turn right from Armagh Street onto quaint Spanish-style New Regent Street, then head back to Cathedral Square, where there are usually buskers, speakers and stalls.

Distance 2.5km (1.5 miles)
Time 1.5 hours plus stops
Start/end point Cathedral Square
Lunch Annie's Wine Bar & Restaurant ($$)
✉ Arts Centre, 2 Worcester Boulevard ☎ 03 365 0566

Around Christchurch

AKAROA AND BANKS PENINSULA

Within days of the British declaring sovereignty over New Zealand in 1840, a shipload of French settlers founded Akaroa on Banks Peninsula southeast of Christchurch, and it has remained French in spirit ever since.

Mountainous Banks Peninsula is a large volcanic outcrop, with the original craters now forming Lyttelton and Akaroa harbours (➤ 145). Allow time for a cruise.

www.akaroa.com

➕ 6S ✉ SH75; 83km (50 miles) from Christchurch 🍴 Several restaurants, especially French 🚍 Day tours available 🛈 Akaroa ☎ 03 304 8600

CHRISTCHURCH GONDOLA

Ride up the side of Mount Cavendish by aerial cable-way from the terminal near the Lyttelton tunnel entrance at Heathcote for a great view over Christchurch and Lyttelton. There is a restaurant and café, a store and a Time Tunnel display at the upper terminal to enjoy once the ride is over.

www.gondola.co.nz

➕ 5S ✉ 10 Bridle Path Road, Christchurch ☎ 03 384 0700 🕐 Daily 10–evening 👣 Moderate 🍴 Summit Café ($$); Pinnacle Restaurant ($$) 🚌 28, 35

FERRYMEAD HERITAGE PARK

This is a living museum of transport and technology, with a working tramway (weekends), railroad and village, plus displays on household appliances, radios, fire engines and aviation. Hundreds of mechanical musical instruments are another draw.

www.ferrymead.org.nz

🚏 5S ✉ 50 Ferrymead Park Drive ☎ 03 384 1970 🕐 Daily 10–4:30

✋ Mon–Fri inexpensive, Sat–Sun and holidays moderate 🚌 35

HANMER SPRINGS

Formerly an alpine spa, this outdoor centre, 135km (84 miles) north of Christchurch, has skiing in winter and adventure options such as jet-boats and bungee jumping. The prime attraction is the **Thermal Pools and Spa,** with its hot pools set in landscaped grounds.

🚏 5R

Thermal Pools and Spa

✉ Amuri Avenue ☎ 03 315 0000; www.hanmersprings.co.nz 🕐 Daily 10–9

✋ Moderate 🍴 Café ($)

INTERNATIONAL ANTARCTIC CENTRE

Located next to the airport and the Operation Deep Freeze base of the United States Air Force, the centre looks at both the geography and the science of the southern polar regions with exhibits and widescreen movies. Some of the highlights are a walk-through polar room (a constant -5°C/23°F), a penguin enclosure and a ride on an Hagglund Antarctic vehicle. There is also a souvenir shop and an interactive room.

www.iceberg.co.nz

🔂 5S 🖂 Orchard Road, Harewood, Christchurch ☎ 03 353 7798 🕓 Oct–Apr daily 9–7; May–Sep 9–5:30 💷 Expensive 🍴 Café ($) 🚍 City Flyer

LYTTELTON

Canterbury's picturesque port, the largest on the South Island, is reached by road either through a tunnel or over the Port Hills. Take a harbour cruise, then walk around the steep, historic streets to the Timeball Station – the timeball was dropped daily from this castellated structure to signal Greenwich Mean Time to ships in the harbour. The Lyttelton Museum has maritime and colonial displays and an Antarctic gallery.

🔂 5S 🖂 SH74; 13km (8 miles) from Christchurch ⛴ Ferry to Diamond Harbour (Banks Peninsula) daily 🚍 28

ℹ️ Anchor Fine Arts, 34 London Street

☎ 03 328 9093; www.lytteltonharbour.co.nz

ORANA WILDLIFE PARK

Animals from New Zealand, Africa, Australia and South America can be seen in this 80ha (200-acre) wildlife park, New Zealand's largest, which specializes in breeding rare and endangered species. There is also a farmyard with domesticated animals, a reptile house, native bird aviaries and a nocturnal kiwi house.

www.oranawildlifepark.co.nz

➕ 5S ✉ McLeans Island Road, Harewood, Christchurch ☎ 03 359 7109 🕐 Daily 10–5; last admission 4:30 🖐 Moderate 🍴 Café ($)

THE TRANZALPINE
Best places to see, ▶ 50–51.

a drive to Akaroa and Banks Peninsula

From Christchurch, the route heads southeast to Banks Peninsula; there are alternatives for the return.

From Cathedral Square, drive south along Colombo Street. After several blocks, turn west (to the right) onto Moorhouse Avenue and follow signs to the left for Akaroa, leading to SH75.

The route leaving the city leads across the coastal plains to Birdlings Flat, skirting Lake Ellesmere, a shallow wetland separated from the sea by the gravelly Kaitorete Spit.

Turn inland to Little River, a former railway terminus.

From here the road climbs steeply up to Hilltop for views over Akaroa Harbour, the crater of an extinct volcano.

The road then drops steeply and follows the harbour round to Akaroa (➤ 140), 83km (51 miles) from Christchurch.

Akaroa's Gallic ancestry is clearly visible in its street names and architecture. In addition to gardens, a museum and a historic lighthouse, a worthwhile attraction is a cruise around the harbour.

The *Black Cat* operates daily at 1:30pm (also 11am Nov–Apr) for a two-hour trip (expensive), often sighting rare Hector's dolphins, penguins and seals.

There are alternative return routes to Christchurch, including the high, narrow Summit Road. Either follow the ridge around to Hilltop, or cross over to follow the route round to Lyttelton Harbour. From there, you can return to Christchurch through the tunnel, along the inland Dyers Pass Road, or via the Evans Pass route to Sumner Beach and along the estuary.

Distance 166km (103 miles)
Time Allow a full day
Start/end point Cathedral Square, Christchurch ✚ 5S
Lunch Harbour Seventy One ($$$) ✉ 71 Beach Road ☎ 03 304 7656

More to see in the Upper South Island

ABEL TASMAN NATIONAL PARK
Best places to see, ➤ 44–45.

KAHURANGI NATIONAL PARK
Largely mountainous and with very few roads through it, the park is known for the Heaphy Track, a 78km (48-mile) walking route. Forest and bush-clad countryside cover the marble and limestone karst country, which is riddled with extensive cave systems.

🕂 4P ✉ Heaphy Track start/end: 28km (17 miles) southwest of Collingwood ☎ 03 546 9339 (Nelson Regional Visitor Centre); www.doc.govt.nz ⊕ Open access to park ✋ Free 🚌 Shuttle transfers arranged locally

KAIKOURA
This small town on the rocky Kaikoura Coast was formerly a whaling station and is now popular as a whale-watching centre. It is also renowned for its crayfish (kaikoura is Maori for 'eat crayfish') and for its spectacular scenery – the inland snow-capped peaks and rocky coast provide numerous opportunities for walks.

www.kaikoura.co.nz

🚹 6Q ✉ SH1; 184km (114 miles) north of Christchurch 🚌 Daily from Christchurch, Blenheim, Picton 🚆 TranzCoastal daily from Christchurch to Picton via Kaikoura and Blenheim (www.tranzscenic.co.nz)

ℹ West End, Kaikoura ☎ 03 319 5641

MARLBOROUGH DISTRICT

The Marlborough district is New Zealand's sunniest region, and as a result the countryside around the town of Blenheim is its premier wine-making region, specializing in sauvignon blanc.

Just outside Blenheim is the **Omaka Aviation Heritage Centre,** which houses one of the world's largest collections of World War I aircraft and has a biennial airshow.

www.destinationmarlborough.com

🚹 5P

ℹ Blenheim Railway Station ☎ 03 577 8080

Omaka Aviation Heritage Centre

✉ 79 Aerodrome Road (signed off SH6, 5km/3 miles west of Blenheim)

☎ 03 579 1305; www.omaka.org.nz 🕐 Daily 10–4 💷 Moderate

🍴 Café ($)

NELSON

The sunny city of Nelson sits in the middle of a rich horticultural, forestry and fishing region. It is also noted for its arts and crafts. Foremost among the city's galleries is the **Suter Art Gallery.** The annual Wearable Art Awards may have moved to Wellington, but the weird and wacky fashions are at **WOW,** the World of WearableArt and Classic Cars Museum.

Paths in the Botanical Reserve lead up to a viewpoint known as the Centre of New Zealand. There is excellent swimming at Tahuna Beach and in the nearby Maitai, Aniseed and Lee rivers.

www.nelsonnz.com

✚ 5P ✉ SH6; 438km (272 miles) north of Christchurch

ℹ Taha o te Awa, 77 Trafalgar Street ☎ 03 546 6228

Suter Art Gallery

✉ 208 Bridge Street ☎ 03 548 4699; www.thesuter.org.nz

🕓 Daily 10:30–4:30 🍴 Café ($) ♿ Inexpensive

WOW

✉ 95 Quarantine Road ☎ 03 547 4573; www.wowcars.co.nz 🕓 Daily 10–5

🍴 Café ($) ♿ Moderate

NELSON LAKES NATIONAL PARK

Inland, south of Nelson, the tiny village of St Arnaud is the main gateway to this mountainous park (102,000ha/252,000 acres), known for its twin lakes of Rotoroa and Rotoiti. Alpine St Arnaud village is on the shores of the latter and is popular for boating, fishing and hiking.

✚ 5Q ✉ Via SH6 and SH63; 119km (74 miles) south of Nelson 🕓 Free access to park 🚌 Bus from Nelson: summer daily; winter on demand (www.nelsonlakesshuttles.co.nz)

ℹ View Road, St Arnaud ☎ 03 521 1806; www.starnaud.co.nz

PICTON AND THE MARLBOROUGH SOUNDS

Picton, at the head of Queen Charlotte Sound, is the commercial focus for the sea inlets formed from the drowned valleys known as

the Marlborough Sounds. In a covered dry dock is the hulk of the 1853 clipper ship *Edwin Fox*, a former carrier of tea, troops, convicts, meat and coal; it is currently being restored. Picton Museum also has an interesting local collection to see.

Launch cruises and fishing trips can be taken around the sounds and there are also walking trails, some requiring several days to complete. There is lodge accommodation on some of the walks, including the renowned Queen Charlotte Track.

www.destinationmarlborough.com

✠ Picton: 5P; Marlborough Sounds: 6N ✉ SH1; 28km (17.5 miles) north of Blenheim 🚢 From Wellington

ℹ The Foreshore, Picton ☎ 03 520 3113

HOTELS

CHRISTCHURCH
The Classic Villa ($$–$$$)
Conveniently located opposite the Arts Centre, this Victorian villa has 12 beautifully decorated rooms and a suite.
✉ 17 Worcester Boulevard ☎ 03 377 7905; www.theclassicvilla.co.nz

The George Hotel ($$$)
The George has 53 deluxe rooms and two restaurants. It has won numerous international awards, not least for its service, with one member of staff to every guest.
✉ 50 Park Terrace ☎ 03 379 4560; www.thegeorge.com

Jailhouse Accommodation ($)
A former prison, complete with window bars, providing excellent accommodation with shared bathrooms.
✉ 338 Lincoln Road, Addington ☎ 03 982 7777; www.jail.co.nz

ABEL TASMAN NATIONAL PARK
Awaroa Lodge ($$$)
This luxurious eco-friendly lodge has 12 suites, 14 rooms and a restaurant that serves food grown in the resort's garden. Access is by air, water-taxi or on foot only.
✉ Awaroa Bay ☎ 03 528 8758; www.awaroalodge.co.nz

KAIKOURA
Anchor Inn Motel ($$–$$$)
One of the best motels in New Zealand. Located on the Kaikoura waterfront, with magnificent views.
✉ 208 The Esplanade ☎ 03 319 5426; www.anchorinn.co.nz

MARLBOROUGH DISTRICT
Antria Boutique Lodge ($$$)
Mediterranean meets Antipodes, with massive neo-Gothic copper front doors, and furnishings from around the world.
✉ 276 Old Renwick Road, Blenheim ☎ 03 579 2191;
www.antria.co.nz

Old Saint Mary's Convent ($$$)

This old convent has been converted into a luxury retreat. The 24ha (60 acres) of grounds are encircled by olive groves and vineyards.

✉ Rapaura Road, Blenheim ☎ 03 570 5700; www.convent.co.nz

NELSON
Te Puna Wai Lodge ($$–$$$)

Magnificent sea views are had from this restored 1857 villa. Choose from a double room or one-bedroom apartment with kitchen downstairs, or the top-floor suite.

✉ Richardson Street, Port Hills ☎ 03 548 7621; www.tepunawai.co.nz

PICTON AND THE MARLBOROUGH SOUNDS
Portage Resort Hotel ($–$$$)

This relaxed Marlborough Sounds resort has 35 rooms plus a pool. There is also a smart restaurant and waterfront café (► 59).

✉ Kenepuru Sound, RD2, Picton ☎ 03 573 4309; www.portage.co.nz

RESTAURANTS

CHRISTCHURCH
Belgian Beer Café Torenhof ($$)

Mussels and crispy fries, washed down with Belgian beer beside the Avon. The café is in part of the historic Canterbury Provincial Council Buildings (► 136).

✉ 88 Armagh Street ☎ 03 377 1007 🕐 Lunch and dinner daily

Caffe Roma ($$)

European-style coffee house with great breakfasts.

✉ 176 Oxford Terrace ☎ 03 379 3879 🕐 Daily 7–4

Cook'n' with Gas ($$$)

Housed in a beautiful Victorian villa opposite the Arts Centre, this restaurant focuses on the best locally available ingredients. Boutique beers feature large, and include a spruce beer brewed to Captain Cook's original recipe.

✉ 23 Worcester Boulevard ☎ 03 377 9166 🕐 Dinner Mon–Sat

Dux de Lux ($$)
See page ➤ 58.

Little India Bistro & Tandoor ($$)
The menu includes excellent dishes from northern India, particularly the Punjab. You can select your preferred heat intensity when you choose your dishes.
✉ Corner of New Regent and Gloucester streets ☎ 03 377 7997 🕐 Lunch Mon–Fri, dinner daily

Pegasus Bay ($$$)
See page ➤ 59.

Strawberry Fare ($$)
Breakfast, brunch and light salad and pasta dishes are served here, but the specialty of the house is its mouthwatering desserts.
✉ 114 Peterborough Street ☎ 03 365 4897 🕐 Mon–Fri 7am–late, Sat–Sun 9am–late

KAIKOURA
Green Dolphin Restaurant and Bar ($$–$$$)
As you would expect from Kaikoura's location and reputation, seafood is a specialty here, along with local beef and lamb.
✉ 12 Avoca Street ☎ 03 319 6666 🕐 Dinner daily

Kaikoura Seafood BBQ ($)
A takeout with a difference, this outdoor set-up serves fresh seafood sandwiches and soups in a stunning seaside setting.
✉ Avoca Street ☎ 027 330 0511 🕐 Daily 10:30–dusk, weather permitting

MARLBOROUGH DISTRICT
Herzog Luxury Restaurant ($$$)
The five-course dégustation and à la carte menus both focus on Mediterranean-style dishes made with local seasonal ingredients. The more relaxed winery bistro is open from mid-Oct to mid-May.
✉ 81 Jeffries Road, Blenheim ☎ 03 572 8770 🕐 Mid-Oct to mid-May lunch and dinner daily

Hotel d'Urville ($$$)

Great food, which makes use of Marlborough Sounds ingredients, gained this hotel a place in the finals of the 2009 *Cuisine* magazine Restaurant of the Year awards.

✉ 52 Queen Street, Blenheim ☎ 03 577 9945 🕔 Dinner daily

Twelve Trees Vineyard Restaurant ($$)

Allan Scott's famous wines are complemented by a lunchtime menu of dishes incorporating local produce. A specialty is the chowder of Marlborough Sounds seafood.

✉ Allan Scott Winery, Jacksons Road, Blenheim ☎ 03 572 9054 🕔 Daily 9–4:30

NELSON
The Boat Shed Café ($$$)

See page ► 58.

Hot Rock Gourmet Pizza Pasta Bar ($$)

Wood-fired pizzas and fresh pasta near the city's beach. The wine list includes local Nelson labels, as well as other New Zealand and Italian vintages.

✉ 8–10 Tahunanui Drive ☎ 03 546 4421 🕔 Dinner daily

Morrison Street Café ($$)

Regular art exhibitions draw an interesting crowd to this lively café. The breakfast and lunch menus are imaginative, accompanied by great coffee.

✉ 244 Hardy Street ☎ 03 548 8110 🕔 Mon–Fri 7:30–4, Sat 8:30–4, Sun 9–4

PICTON
Gusto ($–$$)

The best place in town for lunch, or for a great cup of coffee. The service is friendly and there's pavement seating in fine weather.

✉ 33 High Street ☎ 03 573 7171 🕔 Daily 7:30–3:30

Portage Resort Hotel ($$$)

See page ► 59.

SHOPPING

Cathedral Square marks the heart of downtown Christchurch, with Colombo Street and Cashel Street being the main shopping areas. To the north of the square there are tourist and souvenir shops, and the visitor information office is situated in Cathedral Square. The largest suburban shopping areas are at Riccarton and Hornby.

DEPARTMENT AND CLOTHING STORES

Ballantynes
Popular department store with a large variety of merchandise.
✉ City Mall, 130 Cashel Street, Christchurch ☎ 03 379 7400

Dress-Smart Outlet Shopping Centre
Designer footwear and clothing at discount prices.
✉ 409 Main South Road, Hornby, Christchurch ☎ 03 349 5750

Swanndri Concept Store
Popular New Zealand brand, best known for bush shirts.
✉ 75 Clarence Street, Riccarton ☎ 03 341 3945

Untouched World
Beautiful sustainably and ethically produced designer clothes.
✉ 301 Montreal Street, Christchurch ☎ 03 962 6551

BOOKS, MAGAZINES AND MUSIC

Everyman Records
Independent retailer selling CDs and vinyls. Also Nelson's main event booking agent.
✉ 249 Hardy Street, Nelson ☎ 03 548 3083

Mapworld
National and provincial maps, atlases and guidebooks.
✉ Corner of Manchester and Gloucester streets ☎ 03 374 5399

Scorpio Books
Mainly, but not exclusively, arts and serious topics.
✉ 79 Hereford Street, Christchurch ☎ 03 379 2882

CRAFTS, ANTIQUES AND MARKETS

Antique Print Gallery
Original and reproduction historic maps and natural history prints.
✉ 34 New Regent Street, Christchurch ☎ 03 379 9869

Arts Centre
Stores selling arts, crafts and souvenirs, and a lively weekend market that's worth a special visit.
✉ 2 Worcester Boulevard, Christchurch ☎ 03 363 2836

Beadz Unlimited
Browse through a huge selection of beads, including some made from paua-shell.
✉ Arts Centre, 2 Worcester Boulevard, Christchurch ☎ 03 379 5126

Nelson Market
Fresh produce, crafts and designer clothes and the chance to mingle with the locals.
✉ Montgomery Square, Nelson ☎ 03 546 6454 🕓 Sat 8–1, Sun 9–1

New Zealand Jade and Opal Centre
High-quality jade carvings, jewellery and superb opals are sold here.
✉ Arts Centre, 2 Worcester Boulevard, Christchurch ☎ 03 377 0956

SOUVENIRS

Arts Centre Leather Shop
Leather bags, belts and boots.
✉ Arts Centre, 2 Worcester Boulevard, Christchurch ☎ 03 366 1143

The Grape Escape
A small complex just outside Nelson that houses a gift shop, natural-fibre boutique, candle shop, and café and wine bar.
✉ Corner of McShane Road and SH60, Nelson ☎ 03 544 3929

Magnificent New Zealand Gifts
A wide range of crafts, knitwear, books and T-shirts.
✉ 216 Hardy Street, Nelson ☎ 03 546 6066

ENTERTAINMENT

CULTURAL ACTIVITIES

Christchurch Town Hall

A concert chamber and theatre with frequent events.

✉ 86–95 Kilmore Street, Christchurch ☎ 03 366 8899;
www.convention.co.nz

Isaac Theatre Royal

This refurbished venue hosts ballet, drama and musicals.

✉ 145 Gloucester Street, Christchurch ☎ 03 366 6326;
www.isaactheatreroyal.co.nz

Ko Tane

Maori cultural performances and a *hangi* meal are held at the
Willowbank wildlife reserve every evening.

✉ Willowbank, Hussey Road, Christchurch ☎ 03 359 6226;
www.kotane.co.nz

NIGHTLIFE

Christchurch Casino

Featuring gaming machines, blackjack, Keno and roulette.

✉ 30 Victoria Street, Christchurch ☎ 03 365 9999

Victorian Rose

A firm supporter of the local music scene, with regular
jazz nights.

✉ 281 Trafalgar Street, Nelson ☎ 03 548 7631

SPORT

Christchurch is renowned for its exciting horse-racing scene,
whose highlight is Cup and Show Week in early November.

An hour outside the city is the popular ski resort of Mt Hutt, and
skiing is also available at smaller fields at Amuri near Hanmer
Springs, Rainbow near Nelson, and Mt Lyford near Kaikoura during
the winter season.

Offshore, Kaikoura's waters are popular with scuba-divers in the
warmer months, as are those of the Marlborough Sounds.

Lower South Island

The lower half of South Island is home to some of New Zealand's most spectacular scenery. Flowing west out of the snowfields of the Southern Alps are the Fox and Franz Josef glaciers, while to the south, beyond more dramatic peaks, is Fiordland. This region of steep-sided inlets and remote forests and lakes is one of the world's largest and most impressive national parks.

Lovers of the great outdoors are always attracted to photogenic Queenstown, on Lake Wakatipu. Within easy reach of fjords and a

centre for skiing and various adventure options for serious thrill-seekers, it is a world-famous holiday destination, and rightly so. South is Invercargill, regional hub of Southland and the main departure point for New Zealand's often forgotten third island, Stewart Island. This island is a true haven for bush wildlife and offers the chance to see animals in their natural environment. The region's other main city is Dunedin. This lively city is renowned for its proud Scottish heritage and for its university.

QUEENSTOWN

The South Island's second-largest lake, Wakatipu, with the Remarkables mountain range as a backdrop, provides a dramatic and picturesque setting for Queenstown on its northeastern shore.

This is undoubtedly New Zealand's premier resort for adventure and action, offering a host of exhilarating activities ranging from jet-boating on the nearby Shotover and Kawarau rivers to helicopter trips over the mountains, from bungee jumping to skiing at Coronet Peak, and from paragliding to white-water rafting.

Less sensational but equally appealing are the gentler pursuits of lake cruising on an old steamboat, hiking, horseback riding and fishing. For those who prefer just to look, there are museums, parks and gardens in and around the town. Not to be missed is the Skyline Gondola (➤ 48) for spectacular views of the lake.

The nightlife here is just as lively, and there are bars, cafés and restaurants and a good range of entertainment. Shoppers and strollers are well catered to, with Church Street and the Mall running down to the waterfront, the focal point of the town. Formerly a gold-mining town, Queenstown has come to rely on tourism since the beginning of the last century and now makes every possible effort to attract visitors from around the world.

www.queenstown-vacation.com

✚ 2W

🛈 Clocktower Building, corner of Shotover and Camp streets

☎ 03 442 4100

TSS *Earnslaw*

The lake steamer TSS *Earnslaw*, built in 1912, operates frequent cruises from its wharf near downtown. This 'lady of the lake' offers local sightseeing trips and excursions to Walter Peak Farm, a high-country sheep station across the lake where sheep-shearing and dog-handling are demonstrated.

✉ Steamer Wharf ☎ 03 249 7416; www.realjourneys.co.nz ⏰ Nov to mid-Apr daily 10, 12, 2, 4, 6, 8; mid-Apr to Oct 12, 2, 4 👋 Expensive 🍴 On-board café ($); 6pm summer cruise can include dinner at Walter Peak ($$$)

Kiwi Birdlife Park

A number of avaries, including some housing endangered species, a native bush area, a nocturnal kiwi house and a replica Maori hunting village are the main attractions here.

www.kiwibird.co.nz

✉ Brecon Street ☎ 03 442 8059 ⏰ Oct–Apr daily 9–7; May–Sep 9–5 (times may vary) 👋 Expensive

Queenstown Gardens

Queenstown Gardens (1867) cover a small promontory jutting into the lake and offer views of the mountains. Williams Cottage, at the entrance to the Gardens, dates from 1865 and is one of Queenstown's oldest buildings; it is now a café and design store.

✉ Marine Parade or Park Street ⏰ Unrestricted access

Skyline Gondola
Best places to see, ➤ 48–49.

Underwater Observatory
At the end of the main pier on Queenstown's
waterfront is this below-lake observatory. Through
the huge windows interested spectators can view
the lake's inhabitants at close quarters, including
trout, eels and scaup (diving ducks).
✉ Rees Street ☎ 03 442 6142 🕐 Daily 8:30–dusk
✋ Inexpensive

Around Queenstown

ARROWTOWN
With its stone cottages and exotic trees, such as
sycamore and oak, this old gold-mining town is
less commercialized than Queenstown. The main
shopping street is lovely to stroll along, and a
visit to the Lakes District Museum and Gallery
is informative.
www.arrowtown.com
✚ 3V ✉ 20km (12.5 miles) from Queenstown
🛈 Lakes District Museum, 49 Buckingham Street
☎ 03 442 1824

CORONET PEAK
Between June and October this is one of the region's
leading ski fields, but it is worth visiting at any time of
the year as the 18km (11-mile) drive from
Queenstown offers sky-high views over Lake
Wakatipu and the surrounding countryside. During
winter a regular bus shuttle operates.
www.nzski.com

2V 18km (11 miles) from Queenstown 03 442 4620 Three cafés ($–$$) and one restaurant ($$$) open in winter Shuttle in ski season

SKIPPERS CANYON

The narrow cliffside road leading 17km (10 miles) to the remnants of Skippers, a former gold-mining township, is the main attraction here, but only experienced drivers should attempt it (rental vehicles are prohibited). For those who would rather be a passenger, several companies offer 4WD tours.

Various adventure activities take place above and along the river, if you're brave enough. The Shotover Canyon Swing involves launching yourself into the canyon from a height of 109m (358ft), while the Shotover Jet is a thrilling jet-boat ride that twists around the river's rocky walls. White-water rafting is also on offer.

2V 28km (17.5 miles) from Queenstown

Nomad Safaris

19 Shotover Street, Queenstown 0800 688 222, 03 442 6699; www.nomadsafaris.co.nz Expensive

Shotover Canyon Swing

37 Shotover Street, Queenstown 0800 729 464, 03 442 6990; www.canyonswing.co.nz Expensive

Shotover Jet

Shotover Jet Beach, Gorge Road, Arthurs Point, Queenstown 0800 746 868, 03 442 8570; www.shotoverjet.com Expensive

Queenstown Rafting

35 Shotover Street, Queenstown 0800 723 8464, 03 442 9792; www.queenstownrafting.co.nz Expensive

a walk in Queenstown

The first part of this stroll around Queenstown is flat, but the second part involves a climb in the countryside.

From the wharf at the foot of the Mall, outside Eichardt's Hotel, walk towards the peninsula jutting into the lake. This short stroll, either along the lake's beach or adjacent footpath, leads to the Queenstown Gardens (▶ 159).

Here, paths lead past flowers and trees, as well as recreational amenities such as tennis courts and a bowling rink. There are views back through the trees to downtown Queenstown or out over the lake. The impressive southeastward view across the lake includes the Remarkables range.

Loop around to the access road (Park Street) and walk up the streets behind Queenstown. Turn left at the top of Sydney Street onto Hallenstein Street, then right onto Edgar and Kent streets.

From here, note the signposted Queenstown Hill Walkway. Follow this path for some 4.5km (2.5 miles), ascending to a height of about 900m (3,000ft). The path passes through bush (mostly exotic trees, including pine and fir), with the vegetation becoming scrubbier at higher altitudes. There are patches of schist rock and a small tarn (lake) on the way. The splendid view opens out over the town, Lake Wakatipu and surrounding mountains to reveal the steep glaciated valleys and mountainsides of the area.

Return by the same route.

Distance 10km (6 miles)
Time 3.5 hours
Start/end point Foot of the Mall ✚ 2W
Lunch The Bathhouse (➤ 180)

More to see in the Lower South Island

AORAKI/MOUNT COOK NATIONAL PARK
Best places to see, ➤ 52–53.

BLUFF
Invercargill's port of Bluff lies below Bluff Hill at the tip of the South Island. A road leads up to a lookout with views across the harbour to Stewart Island (➤ 174). SH1 terminates at land's end at Stirling Point, with its much-photographed signpost .
www.bluff.co.nz

➕ 3Y ✉ SH1; 27km (16.5 miles) south of Invercargill
ℹ 108 Gala Street, Invercargill ☎ 03 214 6243

CATLINS
This coastal strip at the southeast corner of the South Island has a spectacular coastline of rugged, lonely beaches, while inland lie tracts of undisturbed forests supporting rare endemic species.
www.catlins.org.nz

➕ 4X ✉ 138km (85.5 miles) east of Invercargill
ℹ 4 Clyde Street, Balclutha ☎ 03 418 0388

CROMWELL
East of Queenstown, in the barren landscape of central Otago, Cromwell was partly rebuilt in the 1980s when the Clutha River was dammed to form Lake Dunstan. The story of the Clyde Dam, and of Cromwell's origins as a gold-mining settlement, is presented in the town's information centre and museum.
www.cromwell.org.nz

➕ 3V ✉ SH6 and SH8; 57km (35.5 miles) from Wanaka 🚌 Scheduled coach services daily from Franz Josef, Christchurch, Queenstown and Dunedin
ℹ 47 The Mall ☎ 03 445 0212

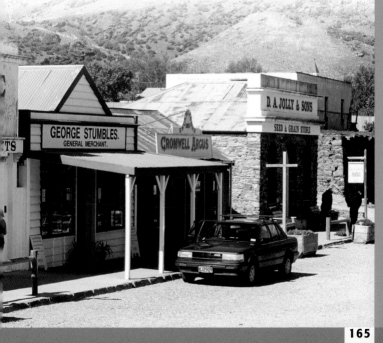

DUNEDIN

The town was founded in 1848 by settlers of the Free Church of
Scotland at the head of Otago Harbour, a long waterway sheltered
by the scenic Otago Peninsula (► 174).

Prosperity soon followed in the wake of the 1860s Otago gold
rush, and the city became New Zealand's wealthiest, leaving a
legacy of handsome, well-preserved buildings. Above all though,
Dunedin is known as a university city (New Zealand's first
university was founded here in 1869), with a lively social, arts and
music scene.

The Octagon, at the heart of the town, is dominated by a statue
to the Scottish poet Robert Burns and the imposing Anglican
St Paul's Cathedral. The fact that the country's only whisky
distillery was located in Dunedin is another reminder of its Scottish
connections.

The extensive botanic gardens (the first to be created in New
Zealand, in 1863) at the northern end of the city include a rose
garden, an aviary, a rhododendron dell (best seen between

October and November), azalea beds and a winter garden glasshouse.
www.dunedinnz.com
⊞ 4W
ℹ 48 The Octagon ☎ 03 474 3300

Hocken Library
The library houses a collection of historic books, early manuscripts, paintings and photographs relating to Otago and the Pacific. General browsing of shelves is not permitted.
✉ Corner of Anzac Avenue and Parry Street
☎ 03 479 8868 🕐 Mon, Wed–Fri 9:30–5, Tue 9:30–9, Sat 9–12 💷 Free
❓ Tours Wed 11, 2

Olveston House
This Jacobean-style mansion, built by the Theomin family in 1906, is furnished as it would have appeared during its early 20th-century heyday. Most of the contents of the house, including a collection of paintings, were gathered during the family's extensive travels overseas.
www.olveston.co.nz
✉ 42 Royal Terrace ☎ 03 477 3320 🕐 Set tours daily: 9:30, 10:45, 12, 1:30, 2:45 and 4 (reservations essential) 💷 Moderate

Otago Museum
Noted for its Maori and Pacific Island sections, the museum also has a comprehensive natural history section, including a re-created Living Tropical Forest, and a maritime exhibition. Discovery World has many scientific hands-on exhibits.
www.otagomuseum.govt.nz
✉ 419 Great King Street ☎ 03 474 7474 🕐 Daily 10–5 💷 Free; Discovery World and Tropical Forest inexpensive

Otago Settlers Museum

This museum tells the story of Otago's social history and includes sections on early Maori habitation and Chinese settlement during the gold-rush era. There is also a photographic gallery of early settler portraits, displayed with furniture and objects from the era. Also housed here is New Zealand's oldest existing steam locomotive (1872).

www.otago.settlers.museum

✉ 31 Queens Gardens ☎ 03 477 5052
🕐 Daily 10–5 ✋ Free

Signal Hill

Located in suburban Opoho, this 393m (1,289ft) peak offers a panorama over central Dunedin. A viewing terrace erected in 1940 marks the centenary of British sovereignty in New Zealand.

✉ End of Signal Hill Road 🕐 Unrestricted

Taieri Gorge Railway

The four-hour return trip to Pukerangi along the craggy Taieri Gorge aboard a diesel-hauled excursion train leaves Dunedin station every day. In addition to the scenery, there are many Victorian bridges and viaducts to admire. Dunedin Railway Station, a grand Edwardian (1906) building with an ornate interior, is a landmark.

www.taieri.co.nz

✉ Dunedin Railway Station, Anzac Avenue ☎ 03 477 4449 🕐 Oct–Apr daily 2:30; Mar–Sep 12:30 ✋ Expensive 🍴 Refreshments on train ($)

FIORDLAND NATIONAL PARK

Best places to see, ➤ 36–37.

FOX AND FRANZ JOSEF GLACIERS

These two huge glaciers, situated some 25km (16 miles) apart, are the main draws of Westland Tai Poutini National Park. They are the only glaciers that descend as low as 300m (1,000ft) above sea level in temperate zones.

Guided tours and hikes onto the glaciers, plus scenic aeroplane and helicopter trips, are available from both Fox and Franz Josef villages. The national park headquarters, which includes a display about the glaciers, is at Franz Josef.

www.glaciercountry.co.nz

✚ 3T ✉ Glaciers: SH6; Franz Josef is 187km (116 miles) from Greymouth
ℹ SH6, Franz Josef ☎ 03 752 0796

HAAST

Situated 117km (72 miles) southwest of Fox Glacier, this settlement marks the entrance to the Haast Pass route. Centred on the UNESCO-designated Southwest New Zealand World Heritage Area, the Haast region includes an extensive area of wetlands, rainforests, coastal lagoons and swamps.

➕ 2U ✉ SH6; 317km (197 miles) southwest of Greymouth 🚌 Daily from the glaciers and Queenstown

ℹ Haast visitor centre ☎ 03 750 0809 🕐 Oct–Apr daily 9–6; May–Sep 9–12:30, 1–4:30

INVERCARGILL

New Zealand's southernmost city lies in a flat pastoral region close to Foveaux Strait. Its main attraction is the **Southland Museum and Art Gallery** in Queens Park, with displays about natural history, colonial settlers and Maori heritage. The museum also has an enclosure housing living specimens of the rare tuatara, and a presentation about the sub-Antarctic islands – five uninhabited rocky clusters lying up to 700km (430 miles) to the south.

www.visitinvercargillnz.com

➕ 3Y

Southland Museum and Art Gallery

✉ Gala Street, Queens Park ☎ 03 219 9069; www.southlandmuseum.com 🕐 Mon–Fri 8:30–5, Sat–Sun 10–5 ✋ Free 🍴 Café ($)

LAKE MANAPOURI AND DOUBTFUL SOUND

The best way to enjoy the beauty of this lake is by taking a cruise. The most popular trip is to West Arm, where an underground hydroelectric power plant has been built. Access to the powerhouse is by coach along a 2km (1-mile) tunnel. Some tours continue across the Wilmot Pass to the remote sea inlet of Doubtful Sound, where another cruise can be taken.

➕ Lake Manapouri: 2X; Doubtful Sound: 1X ✉ South of Te Anau ☎ 03 249 6602; www.realjourneys.co.nz 🕐 West Arm: Oct–Apr daily 12:30. Doubtful

Sound (day): 27 Dec–early Mar 8:30–9:45, 11:30; early Mar–end Mar and mid-Nov to 26 Dec 8:30, 9:45; rest of year 9:45. Doubtful Sound (overnight): Sep–May 12 or 12:30

LAKE TEKAPO

Accessible from the main road between Christchurch and Mount Cook Village (SH8), the lake lies at the northern end of the Mackenzie Country basin. Glacial deposits account for the amazing milky turquoise colour of the water.

A picturesque stone chapel on the edge of the lake, built in 1935, is a favourite tourist stop. Alpine flights are also available.

✚ 3T ✉ SH8; 226km (140 miles) southwest of Christchurch 🚌 Daily from Christchurch and Queenstown

ℹ Lake Tekapo Visitor centre ☎ 03 680 6686

MILFORD SOUND

Best places to see, ➤ 36–37.

a drive from Queenstown to Milford Sound

Whether undertaken by rental car or coach, the most popular road tour from Queenstown is the round trip to Milford Sound (➤ 36). Allowing time for a cruise on the fjord, it is a 12-hour day.

From Queenstown, drive 7km (4 miles) round to Frankton on SH6A to join SH6, southbound.

The road winds around the bluffs above Lake Wakatipu, passing Kingston at its southern end before rising over a crest to enter farmland.

The road leads to Lumsden to pick up SH94 west, but follow the signposted short cut via SH97 at Five Rivers.

From Mossburn, the road crosses progressively more barren countryside. Note a loop road to Manapouri before arriving at Te Anau (➤ 175).

From Te Anau, SH94 turns northwards, then runs parallel with Lake Te Anau and enters the beech forest of the Eglinton Valley. As the mountains close in, the Divide is crossed into the upper Hollyford Valley and the road climbs up to the Homer Tunnel. On emerging, the road zigzags down to Milford Sound, where a hotel, an airstrip and other facilities have been built. The road ends here. The return is via the same route, although tours also offer coach/fly options.

A cruise on the fjord, with its high, steep sides and waterfalls, is recommended. The facilities at Milford are limited, but basic accommodation and a café are available.

In winter (June to August) the road is prone to snow and there is a risk of avalanches (call 0900 33 222 to check).

Distance 291km (180 miles) each way
Time A 12-hour day with stops
Start/end point Downtown Queenstown ✚ 2W
Lunch Blue Duck Café and Bar ($–$$) ✉ Milford Sound ☎ 03 249 7931

MILFORD TRACK

Often described as 'the finest walk in the world', this four-day, 54km (34-mile) hike runs from the top of Lake Te Anau to Milford Sound. Boat access is required at both ends, and walkers can choose either to travel independently, overnighting in park huts, or join a fully guided trip. Both options require advance reservations.

✚ 2W ☎ 03 249 8514 for reservations; www.doc.govt.nz ✋ Expensive

OTAGO PENINSULA

The craggy peninsula guarding Dunedin's harbour is renowned for its wildlife. There are several reserves on the peninsula, but the most special is the **Royal Albatross Centre** at Taiaroa Head, the only mainland breeding colony for giant royal albatrosses in the world. The colony has a special viewing gallery. Also on view here is the world's only fully restored Armstrong disappearing gun.

The peninsula is also home to **Larnach Castle,** built in 1871, complete with ballroom and battlements. The castle has been renovated and is open to view and offers accommodation.

✚ 5W

Royal Albatross Centre

✉ Harrington Point Road ☎ 03 478 0499 (bookings essential); www.albatross.org.nz
🕐 Tours 24 Nov–Easter daily 9–7 every 30 mins; rest of year from 10 every hour (closing time varies). Viewing observatory closed 17 Sep–23 Nov but tours of gun still available ✋ Expensive 🍴 Café ($)

Larnach Castle

✉ Camp Road ☎ 03 476 1616; www.larnachcastle.co.nz 🕐 Daily 9–5 ✋ Moderate 🍴 Café ($)

STEWART ISLAND AND RAKIURA NATIONAL PARK

New Zealand's third-largest island, covering 1,746sq km (674sq miles), lies 27km (16.5 miles) south of the South Island. It can be

reached by air from Invercargill or by catamaran from Bluff.
Although there are few roads, there are good walking trails,
including the arduous 10-day North-West Circuit.
www.stewartisland.co.nz

🚻 3Z 🚢 Foveaux Express catamaran (☎ 03 212 7660;
www.stewartislandexperience.co.nz)

❌ Stewart Island Flights (☎ 03 218 9129; www.stewartislandflights.com)

🚹 12 Elgin Terrace, Halfmoon Bay ☎ 03 219 1400

TE ANAU
Gateway to Fiordland National Park (▶ 36–37), the township
beside Lake Te Anau is the starting point for many walking trails and
boat cruises. One of the latter takes visitors to the **Te Anau
Glowworm Caves**. At the Te Anau Wildlife Centre you can see the
takahe, a flightless bird believed to be extinct until 1948.

🚻 2X

🚹 Lakefront Drive, Te Anau ☎ 03 249 8900; www.fiordland.org.nz

Te Anau Glowworm Caves

✉ Real Journeys, corner of Town Centre and Mokonui streets ☎ 03 249
7416; www.realjourneys.co.nz 🕐 Oct–Apr daily 2, 5:45, 7, 8:15; May–Sep
2, 7 ✋ Expensive

TWIZEL AND LAKE PUKAKI

The road from Twizel to Mount Cook Village (➤ 53) runs alongside the glacier-fed Lake Pukaki, known for its distinctive blue colouring. Built in 1968 as a service town for the Upper Waitaki hydroelectricity scheme, it now serves the tourist industry.

✚ 3U ✉ SH8; 284km (176 miles) southwest of Christchurch 🚌 Daily from Christchurch and Queenstown

ℹ Twizel Events Centre

☎ 03 435 3124; www.twizel.com

WANAKA

Forming the eastern gateway to South Westland via the Haast Pass, Wanaka is on the shores of Lake Wanaka. The town has skiing in season and is the main base for Mount Aspiring National Park. In town are mazes and illusions at **Puzzling World.** The **New Zealand Fighter Pilots Museum** hosts the large biennial Warbirds Over Wanaka airshow.

✚ 3V ℹ The Log Cabin, Lakefront, 100 Ardmore Street, Wanaka

☎ 03 443 1233; www.lakewanaka.co.nz

ℹ Mount Aspiring National Park Centre: 03 443 7660

Puzzling World

✉ SH84 (main Queenstown road) ☎ 03 443 7489; www.puzzlingworld.co.nz

🕐 Oct–Apr daily 8:30–5:30; May–Sep 8:30–5 🍴 Café ($; with separate entrance) ♿ Inexpensive

New Zealand Fighter Pilots Museum

✉ Wanaka Airport, SH6 ☎ 03 443 7010; www.nzfpm.co.nz 🕐 Daily 9–4

♿ Inexpensive; Warbirds Over Wanaka: expensive

WESTLAND TAI POUTINI NATIONAL PARK

Exploring, ➤ 169, Fox and Franz Josef glaciers.

WHITE HERON SANCTUARY

Amid the lagoons that lie on the northern fringes of Westland Tai Poutini National Park is New Zealand's only breeding site for the white heron. These majestic birds nest between October and early March, during which time tours may be taken to see them. Tours leave from Whataroa.

✚ 3T ✉ Whataroa; 140km (87 miles) south of Greymouth

☎ Tours: 03 753 4120; www.whiteherontours.co.nz ⬤ Access controlled

✋ Expensive 🚌 Daily from Greymouth, Nelson, and Fox and Franz Josef townships

HOTELS

QUEENSTOWN
Eichardt's Private Hotel ($$$)
This centrally located historic hotel was founded in 1866, and caters to the luxury boutique market.

✉ Marine Parade ☎ 03 441 0450; www.eichardtshotel.co.nz

Heritage Queenstown ($$–$$$)
On the western edge of town in a quiet location, the Heritage has great views. There is a restaurant and bar with open fire.

✉ 91 Fernhill Road ☎ 03 442 4988; www.heritagehotels.co.nz

Queenstown House ($$$)
A well-established modern upper-range bed-and-breakfast.

✉ 69 Hallenstein Street ☎ 03 442 9043; www.queenstownhouse.co.nz

YHA Queenstown Lakefront ($)
Set on Lake Wakatipu, with views to the Remarkables and only 10 minutes' walk from town. Single, double/twin and dormitory rooms.

✉ 88–90 Lake Esplanade ☎ 03 442 8413; www.yha.co.nz

AORAKI/MOUNT COOK
The Hermitage ($$–$$$)
Spectacularly situated among the peaks of the Southern Alps, this is one of New Zealand's most famous hotels.

✉ Mount Cook Village ☎ 03 435 1809; www.mount-cook.com

DUNEDIN
The Brothers Boutique Hotel ($$–$$$)
This former home of the Christian Brothers Order, close to the Octagon, has been refurbished to provide 15 comfortable rooms.

✉ 295 Rattray Street ☎ 03 477 0043; www.brothers.co.nz

Corstorphine House Private Hotel ($$$)
A listed 1863 heritage building, this neoclassical private hotel is surrounded by an estate and has fine views across the city.

✉ 23A Milburn Street, Caversham ☎ 03 487 1000; www.corstorphine.co.nz

Southern Cross ($$–$$$)

Dunedin's premier hotel, located in the heart of the city centre, dates back to 1883. It has three in-house restaurants, a bar and a fitness centre.

✉ Corner of Princes and High streets ☎ 03 477 0752; www.scenic-circle.co.nz

INVERCARGILL
Ascot Park Hotel ($$–$$$)

Large and modern, the city's top hotel is located in park-like surroundings on the outskirts of Invercargill.

✉ Corner of Tay Street and Racecourse Road ☎ 03 217 6195; www.ascotparkhotel.co.nz

TE ANAU
Fiordland Lodge ($$$)

A purpose-built luxury lodge in the classic style, this has stunning views across the lake and mountains.

✉ 472 Te Anau–Milford Highway ☎ 03 249 7832; www.fiordlandguides.co.nz

WANAKA
Cardrona Hotel ($$)

This hotel may be a little out of the way, but it's well worth the journey – it's more than 140 years old and retains much of its original character. Reservations are essential.

✉ Crown Range Road ☎ 03 443 8153; www.cardronahotel.co.nz

WESTLAND NATIONAL PARK
Te Weheka Inn ($$$)

This modern purpose-built two-floor inn is highly rated, and has spacious bedrooms.

✉ SH6, Fox Glacier ☎ 03 751 0730; www.weheka.co.nz

Rainforest Retreat ($–$$$)

Log cabins nestle among the trees in a quiet bush setting.

✉ Cron Street, Franz Josef ☎ 03 752 0220; www.rainforestretreat.co.nz

RESTAURANTS

QUEENSTOWN

The Bathhouse ($$–$$$)

A showcase of modern New Zealand cuisine served in a Victorian former bathhouse on the beach.

✉ 15–28 Marine Parade ☎ 03 442 5625 ◷ Tue–Sun 10–5, 6–late

The Bunker ($$$)

Top-notch food is created by Head Chef Gwen Harvie in this small restaurant and cocktail bar tucked away in central Queenstown.

✉ Cow Lane ☎ 03 441 8030 ◷ Dinner daily

Dux de Lux ($$)

Boutique beers, vegetarian dishes and seafood in the Queenstown branch of the Christchurch restaurant.

✉ 14–16 Church Street ☎ 03 442 9688 ◷ Daily 11am–late

Flame Bar and Grill ($$)

Expertly cooked chargrilled steaks, ribs and burgers for meat-lovers. And there's the bonus of awesome views across the lake to the Remarkables.

✉ 61 Beach Street ☎ 03 409 2342 ◷ Lunch Jan–Feb and Jul–Aug daily, dinner daily

Gantley's ($$$)

This restaurant, housed in a renovated out-of-town historic stone building, has a well-deserved reputation for good food and service.

✉ 172 Arthurs Point Road ☎ 03 442 8999 ◷ Dinner daily

Gibbston Valley Winery ($$)

Delicious lunches at one of the world's southernmost vineyards.

✉ SH6, 24km (15 miles) east of Queenstown ☎ 03 442 6910 ◷ Lunch daily

Luciano's ($$)

A restaurant with a gangster theme, dishing up sourdough pizzas, pasta and other Italian fare.

✉ Steamer Wharf ☎ 03 409 2460 ◷ Dinner daily

Minami Jujisei ($$)

A long-established Japanese restaurant serving a range of dishes, from sushi and sashimi to tempura and chicken yakitori. It also has a sushi bar and private dining room.

✉ 45 Beach Street ☎ 03 442 9854 🕒 Lunch Mon–Sat, dinner daily

Vesta ($)

Light lunches, snacks and coffees are served in one of Queenstown's oldest cottages, which also doubles as a cool design store.

✉ Williams Cottage, Queenstown Gardens ☎ 03 442 5687
🕒 Mon–Sat 10–6

ARROWTOWN

Saffron ($$$)

Fresh seasonal ingredients enhance the award-winning menu, from Stewart Island scampi to chargrilled venison.

✉ 18 Buckingham Street ☎ 03 442 0131 🕒 Lunch and dinner daily

DUNEDIN

Bell Pepper Blues ($$$)

Chef Michael Coughlin has been treating Dunedin's residents to award-winning food since 1992. Specialties are the venison and Coughlin's sumptuous desserts, which include a delicate raspberry cream-cheese mousse.

✉ 474 Princes Street ☎ 03 474 0973 🕒 Dinner Tue–Sat

Etrusco ($$)

Pasta and pizza are served upstairs in a beautiful heritage building with stained-glass windows, stucco ceilings and a wooden floor.

✉ 8A Moray Place ☎ 03 477 3737 🕒 Dinner daily

Plato ($$)

A relaxed eatery in a former seafarers' hostel. The best place in the city for Sunday brunch.

✉ 2 Birch Street ☎ 03 477 4235 🕒 Brunch Sun from 11am,
dinner daily

Speight's Ale House Bar & Restaurant ($–$$)

On the historic site of the original Speight's brewery (tours daily), this relaxed bar and restaurant serves hearty meals.

✉ 200 Rattray Street ☎ 03 471 9050 🕐 Daily 11:30–late

INVERCARGILL
Bluff Drunken Sailor Café Bar ($–$$)

Choice of snacks or meals at this southernmost point. Oysters and clam chowder are specialties.

✉ 8 Ward Parade, Bluff ☎ 03 212 8855 🕐 Daily 11:30–3, dinner Sat

Cabbage Tree Restaurant and Outpost Tavern ($$)

Choose from a huge menu of pub-style dishes in this tavern west of the city, popular for being good value.

✉ 379 Dunns Road, Otatara ☎ 03 213 1443 🕐 Daily 10am–late

MOUNT COOK
Panorama Room ($$$)

The panorama of this restaurant's name refers to its stunning views of Aoraki/Mount Cook. The focus here is on New Zealand ingredients, which feature in such dishes as pan-fried scallops with salmon caviar and navarin of lamb.

✉ Mount Cook Village ☎ 03 435 1809 🕐 Dinner daily

TE ANAU
Redcliff Café and Bar ($$)

A lively bar and restaurant with a menu that focuses on wild game and seafood dishes.

✉ 12 Mokonui Street, Te Anau ☎ 03 249 7431 🕐 Dinner daily. Closed Jul

WANAKA
Amigos ($$)

Casual Mexican fare using local corn-fed free-range chicken and Southland beef. The bar staff mix the meanest margaritas in town.

✉ 34a Ardmore Street ☎ 03 443 7872 🕐 Daily from 5pm

Botswana Butchery ($$$)

Botswana Butchery serves a wide range of expertly wood-grilled or pan-fried steaks, as well as game and seafood dishes using New Zealand ingredients.

✉ 33 Ardmore Street ☎ 03 443 6745 🕐 Daily 12–11

The Cow Restaurant ($$)

Great-tasting pizzas and pasta dishes, in front of a roaring fire in winter.

✉ Post Office Lane, off Ardmore Street ☎ 03 443 4269 🕐 Daily 12–12

Missy's Kitchen ($$)

New Zealand ingredients are given a Mediterranean flavour in such dishes as Cardrona lamb shoulder stuffed with olive tapenade, and potato gnocchi with rabbit ragout. Enjoy the lake and mountain views from the balcony or in winter sit inside by the fire.

✉ Corner of Ardmore Street and Lakeside Drive ☎ 03 443 5099 🕐 Dinner daily

WESTLAND TAI POUTINI NATIONAL PARK

Beeches ($$)

Has a varied menu that includes whitebait patties, a specialty of the West Coast region.

✉ SH6, Franz Josef ☎ 03 752 0721 🕐 Daily 10am–late

SHOPPING

Queenstown is a major tourist attraction and most shops in its compact downtown area are geared towards visitors. It is also the only place in New Zealand where major stores and boutiques stay open until 10pm daily.

Dunedin has many good shops in George and Princes streets, on either side of the Octagon reserve.

Invercargill has a modest downtown shopping area, while the small towns of Te Anau and Wanaka have fairly limited shopping, but enough to interest the visiting browser.

DEPARTMENT AND CLOTHING STORES

Alta
Ski and snowboarding clothes and gear for sale and hire.
✉ 45 Camp Street, Queenstown ☎ 03 442 9330

Arthur Barnett Ltd
A traditional department store where you can find everything from ladies' and men's clothing to household furnishings and giftware.
✉ Meridian Mall, 285 George Street, Dunedin ☎ 03 477 1129

Outside Sports
Everything for the active, including skiing, mountain-biking, hiking and camping gear to purchase or hire.
✉ Shotover Street, Queenstown ☎ 03 441 0074

WoolPress
New Zealand-label clothing, including knitwear and accessories, for men, women and children.
✉ 40 Buckingham Street, Arrowtown ☎ 03 442 1355

ART

Bellamy Gallery
Lively Otago landscapes in watercolour and oil.
✉ 495 Portobello Road, Macandrew Bay, Otago Peninsula ☎ 03 476 1600

Queenstown Gallery
Exclusively New Zealand artworks are sold at this quality gallery.
✉ 61 Beach Street, Queenstown ☎ 03 441 1366

SOUVENIRS

Alpine Artifacts
Choose from a variety of local souvenirs to take home with you.
✉ 34 The Mall, Queenstown ☎ 03 442 8649

Hides
Souvenirs, plus possum, wool and sheepskin jackets.
✉ 185 George Street, Dunedin ☎ 03 477 8927

The Scottish Shop
The place in Dunedin to buy all things Scottish.
✉ 17 George Street, Dunedin ☎ 03 477 9965

ENTERTAINMENT

CULTURAL ACTIVITIES

Regent Theatre
A beautifully restored 1920s theatre with state-of-the-art facilities.
✉ 17 The Octagon, Dunedin ☎ 03 477 8597

NIGHTLIFE

SkyCity Queenstown Casino
Table games and 80-plus gaming machines.
✉ 16–24 Beach Street, Queenstown ☎ 03 441 0400

Surreal
One of Queenstown's popular nightspots, with live music and DJs.
✉ 7 Rees Street, Queenstown ☎ 03 441 8492

SPORT

Fishing
The rivers of southern South Island are renowned for their salmon and trout fishing; a licence is required (www.fishandgame.org.nz).

Horse trekking
Otago is ideal country to explore on horseback. There are numerous operators in the region, including Dart Stables at Glenorchy (www.dartstables.com), which runs tours ranging from two-hour novice treks to overnight expeditions.

Skiing
Coronet Peak (➤ 160–161) and the Remarkables are Queenstown's major ski-fields (www.nzski.com), although you can also find additional ski-fields and facilities at nearby Wanaka (www.skilakewanaka.com).

Index

Acknowledgements

The Automobile Association would like to thank the following photographers, companies and picture libraries for their assistance in the preparation of this book.

Abbreviations for the picture credits are as follows – (t) top; (b) bottom; (c) centre; (l) left; (r) right; (AA) AA World Travel Library.

4l Akaroa Heritage path, AA/A Belcher; **4c** Water Taxi, AA/M Langford; **4r** Hooker Valley, AA/M Langford; **5l** Jet boat, AA/A Reisinger and V Meduna; **5r** Marlborough Sounds, AA/P Kenward; **6/7** Akaroa Heritage Path, AA/A Belcher; **8/9** Lake Taupo, AA/A Belcher; **10** Kapiti Coast, AA/P Kenward; **10/1t** Whale, AA/P Kenward; **10/1b** Waitangi National Reserve, AA/P Kenward; **12** Restaurant, AA/M Langford; **13t** seafood billboard, AA/ M Langford; **13c** Cafe, AA/M Langford; **13b** Kiwi fruit, AA/P Kenward; **14t** Blackberry pie, AA/ P Kenward; **14b** Beer, AA/ M Langford; **15** Café, AA/ M Langford; **16** Walkers, AA/ M Langford; **16/7** Campfire, AA/A Reisinger and V Meduna; **17** Rotorua, AA/A Belcher; **18** Rugby, AA/ P Kenward; **18/9** Piha Beach, AA/ M Langford; **19t** Skippers Canyon, AA/A Reisinger and V Meduna; **19bl** Maori warrior, AA/P Kenward; **19br** Glass of wine, AA/M Langford; **20/1** Water Taxi, AA/M Langford; **24/5** Jazz Festival, AA/M Langford; **27** Bus stop, AA/M Langford; **28t** Taxi, AA/M Langford; **28b** Penguin sign, AA/P Kenward; **29** ATM, AA/M Langford; **30** Telephone box, AA/M Langford; **31** Policeman, AA/A Belcher; **34/5** Hooker Valley, AA/M Langford; **36** Milford Sound, AA/A Belcher; **36/7** Milford Sound, AA/P Kenward; **38** Chateau Tongariro, AA/ M Langford; **38/9** Tongariro National Park, AA/P Kenward; **40/1** Te Papa Museum, AA/A Belcher; **41** Te Papa MuseumPhotolibrary; **42** Maori children, AA/ A Belcher; **42/3** Whakarewarewa Thermal reserve, AA/M Langford; **43** Whakarewarewa Thermal reserve, AA/A Belcher; **44** Water Taxi, AA/M Langford; **44** Hikers, AA/P Kenward; **44/5** Beach, Alamy; **45** Cormorant, AA/M Langford; **46/7** Cape Reinga, AA/P Kenward; **48/9** Skyline Gondala Station, AA/P Kenward; **50** Tranz Alpine Express, AA/A Belcher; **50/1** Arthur's Pass, AA/A Belcher; **52** Mount Cook National Park, AA/M Langford; **52/3** Mount Cook National Park, AA/M Langford; **53** Mount Cook National Park, AA/M Langford; **54/5t** Waitomo Caves, AA/M Langford; **54/5b** Waitomo Caves, AA/M Langford; **56/7** Shotover Gorge, AA/A Reisinger and V Meduna; **58/9** Restaurant, AA/M Langford; **60/1** Mount Cook National Park, AA/M Langford; **62/3** Hooker Valley, AA/M Langford; **64/5** Cable car, AA/A Belcher; **66/7** Aquarium, AA/M Langford; **68/9** Mount Cook, Alamy; **70/1** Marlborough Sounds, AA/P Kenward; **73** Sky Tower, AA/M Langford; **74** Albert Park, AA/A Belcher; **74/5** View from Sky Tower, AA/A Belcher; **76/7** View from North Head, AA/M Langford; **78/9** Auckland Harbour Bridge, AA/A Belcher; **79b** Kelly Tarlton's Underwater World, AA/P Kenward; **80** One Tree Hill, Alamy; **80/1b** Museum of Transport, AA/P Kenward; **81** Maritime Museum, AA/A Belcher; **82/3** Botanical Gardens, AA/M Langford; **83** Rangitoto Island, AA/M Langford; **84** Signs, AA/P Kenward; **84/5** Ferry Building, AA/M Langford; **86** KeriKeri, AA/A Belcher; **86/7** Bay of Islands, AA/A Belcher; **88/9** Waitangi National Reserve, AA/A Belcher; **90** Maori warrior, AA/P Kenward; **91** Rotorua, AA/M Langford; **92** Church in Ohinemutu, AA/P Kenward; **92/3** Rainbow Springs, AA/P Kenward; **94** Waimangu Volcanic Valley, AA/M Langford; **94/5** Wai O Tapu Thermal Wonderland, AA/M Langford; **96** Huka Falls, AA/P Kenward; **97** Taupo, AA/A Belcher; **109** Hawkes Bay, AA/P Kenward; **110** Te Papa Museum, AA/P Kenward; **111** Flowers, AA/P Kenward; **112/3t** Cathedral, AA/P Kenward; **112/3b** Parliament building, AA/A Belcher; **114/5** Kapiti Coast, AA/M Langford; **116** Fern, Pukaha Mount Bruce, D Smith/Robert Harding; **117t** Karori Wildlife Sanctuary, Alamy; **117b** Karori Wildlife Sanctuary, Alamy; **118/9** Oriental Bay, AA/A Belcher; **120/1t** Napier, AA/P Kenward; **120/1b** Cape Kidnappers, AA/P Kenward; **121** Hawkes Bay, AA/M Langford; **122/3** Pukekura Park, AA/P Kenward; **133** Christchurch, AA/M Langford; **134/5** Christchurch, AA/P Kenward; **136** Canterbury Museum, Alamy; **136/7** Christchurch, AA/P Kenward; **137** Tram, AA/M Langford; **139** Cathedral, AA/M Langford; **140** Akaroa, AA/A Belcher; **141** Hanmer Springs, AA/P Kenward; **142/3** Lyttelton, AA/A Belcher; **144** Scenic views of Christchurch, AA/A Belcher; **145** Summit Road, AA/M Langford; **146/7** Whale, AA/P Kenward; **148** Nelson, AA/M Langford; **148/9** The Edwin Fox wreck, AA/M Langford; **149** Queens Charlotte Sound, AA/M Langford; **157** Fiordland National Park, AA/P Kenward; **158/9** Queenstown, AA/P Kenward; **160/1** Arrowtown, AA/A Belcher; **162/3** Botanical Gardens, AA/P Kenward; **164** Bluff, AA/M Langford; **164/5** Cromwell, AA/M Langford; **165** Cromwell, AA/M Langford; **166** Dunedin, AA/ Belcheer; **167** Dunedin, AA/P Kenward; **168** Otago Settlers Museum, Alamy; **169** FranzJosef Glacier, Alamy; **170/1** Lake Manapouri, AA/P Kenward; **171** Lake Tekapo, AA/M Langford; **172/3** Milford Sound, AA/P Kenward; **174** Royal Albatross, AA/P Kenward; **174/5** Stewart Island, AA/M Langford; **176/7** Wanaka, AA/M Langford.

Every effort has been made to trace the copyright holders, and we apologise in advance for any accidental errors. We would be happy to apply the corrections in the following edition of this publication.

Sight locator list

This index relates to the maps on the covers. We have given map references to the main sights of interest in the book. Grid references in italics indicate sights featured on town maps. Some sights within towns may not be plotted on the maps.

 **Questionnaire**

Dear Traveler

Your comments, opinions and recommendations are very important to us.
So please help us to improve our travel guides by taking a few minutes to
complete this simple questionnaire.

Send to: Essential Guides,
MailStop 64, 1000 AAA Drive, Heathrow, FL 32746–5063

Your recommendations...

We always encourage readers' recommendations for restaurants, nightlife
or shopping – if your recommendation is added to the next edition of the
guide, we will send you a FREE AAA Essential Guide of your choice.
Please state below the establishment name, location and your reasons for
recommending it.

_____

_____

_____

_____

Please send me AAA Essential _____

About this guide...

Which title did you buy?

_____ **AAA Essential**

Where did you buy it? _____

When? <u>m m</u> / <u>y y</u>

Why did you choose a AAA Essential Guide? _____

_____

_____

Did this guide meet with your expectations?

Exceeded ☐   Met all ☐   Met most ☐   Fell below ☐

Please give your reasons _____

_____

_____

_____

continued on next page…

Were there any aspects of this guide that you particularly liked? _____
_____
_____
_____
_____
_____

Is there anything we could have done better? _____
_____
_____
_____
_____
_____

About you...
Name (Mr/Mrs/Ms) _____

Address _____
_____
_____ Zip _____

Daytime tel nos. _____

Which age group are you in?
Under 25 ☐   25–34 ☐   35–44 ☐   45–54 ☐   55–64 ☐   65+ ☐

How many trips do you make a year?
Less than one ☐   One ☐   Two ☐   Three or more ☐

Are you a AAA member?   Yes ☐   No ☐
Name of AAA club _____

About your trip
When did you book? m m / y y   When did you travel? m m / y y

How long did you stay? _____

Was it for business or leisure? _____

Did you buy any other travel guides for your trip?   Yes ☐   No ☐
If yes, which ones? _____

Thank you for taking the time to complete this questionnaire.